A Functional Approach to Group Work in Occupational Therapy

A Functional Approach to Group Work in Occupational Therapy

Margot C. Howe, Ed.D., OTR, FAOTA
Professor of Occupational Therapy
Tufts University–Boston School of Occupational Therapy
Medford, Massachusetts

Sharan L. Schwartzberg, Ed.D., OTR
Associate Professor of Occupational Therapy
Tufts University–Boston School of Occupational Therapy
Medford, Massachusetts

 PHILADELPHIA   London   New York   São Paulo
                                  Mexico City   St. Louis   Sydney

J. B. LIPPINCOTT COMPANY

Acquisitions Editor: Lisa A. Biello
Sponsoring Editor: Sanford J. Robinson
Manuscript Editor: Leslie E. Hoeltzel
Indexer: Deana Fowler
Design Director: Tracy Baldwin
Design Coordinator: Anne O'Donnell
Designer: Susan A. Caldwell
Production Supervisor: Kathleen P. Dunn
Production Coordinator: Carol A. Florence
Compositor: International Computaprint Corporation
Printer/Binder: R. R. Donnelley & Sons Company

6 5 4 3 2

**Library of Congress Cataloging
in Publication Data**

Howe, Margot C.
    A functional approach to group work in
    occupational therapy.
    Bibliography: p.
    Includes index.
    1. Occupational therapy.   2. Group work.
I. Schwartzberg, Sharan L.   II. Title.
RM735.H68   1986   615.8'515   85-10370
ISBN 0-397-50657-0

The authors and publisher have exerted every effort to
ensure that drug selection and dosage set forth in this
text are in accord with current recommendations and
practice at the time of publication. However, in view of
ongoing research, changes in government regulations,
and the constant flow of information relating to drug
therapy and drug reactions, the reader is urged to
check the package insert for each drug for any change
in indications and dosage and for added warnings and
precautions. This is particularly important when the
recommended agent is a new or infrequently employed
drug.

To our students,
whose interest and response inspired
our continued study of group work.

Foreword

In the 1930s, Kurt Lewin pioneered a new approach to the study of groups. His work opened the way to a fresh sensitivity and a keener insight into what actually happens when small groups of human beings interact. In the 1940s, Lewin's initiative was developed further, by Kenneth Benne—the co-inventor of the T-group (or Training group)—and others. Benne was also a co-founder of NTL (National Training Laboratories), which became the foremost vehicle for transmitting and refining this new knowledge about the problems, issues, and possibilities of group interaction. It was at Boston University's Human Relations Center, as well as through the NTL, in the 1960s that I had the good fortune to work with Benne at the height of his powers. It was also at Boston University in the 1970s that I first met the authors of this book and shared with them, as their teacher, some of my knowledge about groups.

What the Lewin–Benne–NTL discoveries promised was that these modes of study of the human group would shed light on the difficult and abiding problem of democratic leadership. How can we find an alternative in a democracy to the pattern of the authoritarian or manipulative Leader and the passive–dependent follower? What this new knowledge showed was that, through the T-group model, we can develop an alternative set of skills, attitudes, and structures. These lead to the enhancement of the personal authority of each individual in the group through group-supported risk-taking and self-assertion. Members of these groups acquire the knowledge and skills of effective face-to-face communication, group collaboration, conflict resolution, team development, consensual decision-making, shared leadership, and group invention and innovation. They learn that there is an alternative to having to choose between being The Leader or a follower, and that people can acquire the competence of interdependent and responsible membership, through which all exercise leadership when appropriate.

Over the past two decades, two major developments have occurred in the refinement and application of these group process findings. First, there has been a steady absorption of these discoveries and related skills into everyday knowledge and practice throughout the industrialized world. Usually, they are applied without the original or any distinctive nomenclature. For example, it is unusual now to find the T-group practiced in its original form. Second, there has been widespread adaptation of the original findings to specialized uses—in eclectic fields such as group psychotherapy, organizational development, and pedagogy, and in particular occupations, such as social work and nursing. Until now, however, its application to the field of occupational therapy has remained fragmentary, partial, and unfulfilled.

Over the past decade, the Tufts University–Boston School of Occupational Therapy has developed a reputation as an outstanding center for research, teaching, and practice in occupational therapy. Two key figures in that development have been Dr. Margot Howe and Dr. Sharan Schwartzberg. When they were students in the program I directed at Boston University in Humanistic and Behavioral Studies (which applied the above findings about group process to issues of pedagogy in public and professional education), it was clear to me that they would make a significant contribution to their professional field. Since that time, I have followed their professional careers with appreciation and admiration.

With this book they enter into a great stream of theoretical and practical development—applying the finding about group process to occupational therapy in a new, unique, and powerful way. The heart of their contribution lies in their ingeniously designed and carefully crafted model of the functional group in occupational therapy. They demonstrate in this important and innovative work that they have sensitively assimilated the learnings from the past—they are worthy descendants of Kurt Lewin—and have applied them creatively to their own professional field.

This is a major contribution to research, training theory, and intervention theory in occupational therapy. I am encouraged and heartened by the creative impact I am confident it will make.

Paul Nash
Providence, Rhode Island

Preface

Groups are a part of peoples' experience, not only in normal or healthy life but also in life interrupted by disease and distress. Because of the potential benefits of group work and its versatility, a variety of professionals use this format in settings as diverse as hospitals, schools, and businesses.

Many books have been written on group process, but most have been directed toward psychotherapy, social case work, or organizational development. None address the unique orientation of occupational therapy, which is skills-oriented, action-oriented, and here-and-now oriented. In teaching group process, occupational therapy educators have had to rely on material developed by other disciplines. As educators, we are concerned with the limitations and biases that this may have brought to the profession's education and practice.

It is our goal to begin to fill this void by writing a book that combines theory, research, and practice and is a model for group work in occupational therapy: a functional approach to group work. Because the model is based on our experience and practice in teaching and in conducting occupational therapy treatment groups, as well as our research on group work, *A Functional Approach to Group Work in Occupational Therapy* is presented from the vantage points of the normal group, the therapeutic group, and the occupational focus group, or functional group.

The material is organized to lead the therapist through the logic of planning, implementing, and evaluating a functional group. The content is not focused on a verbal, insight-oriented approach to group work; rather, we explain the functional group as a method to aid individuals in adaptation to their life roles and tasks through the *doing* or *action* in a group. The model we propose is an approach designed for people with physical, social, emotional, or developmental problems and one that primarily stems from occupational therapy philosophy and practice.

Margot C. Howe, Ed.D., OTR, FAOTA
Sharan L. Schwartzberg, Ed.D., OTR

Medford, Massachusetts
January 1985

Acknowledgments

A book such as *A Functional Approach to Group Work in Occupational Therapy* is not conceptualized or completed without contributions from many people. We wish to thank Anne Briggs and Linda Duncombe for their help in the initial stages of the book; Virginia Drachman, Paul Nash, and Kathlyn Reed for their welcome expertise in model development and historical analysis; the Tufts University–Boston School of Occupational Therapy and the Towne House Creative Living Center for the use of their photographs; Glenda Wong for her assistance in drawing; Laura Goldberg for her patience and skill in typing the manuscript; and, finally, Everest and Jennings for their generous and vital support that allowed us to research and develop a model for occupational therapy group work, and S & S Arts and Crafts, Rolyan Medical Products, and the Mabel Louise Riley Research Fund of Tufts University–Boston School of Occupational Therapy for their financial contributions.

Contents

Group Work and the Functional Group Model

The recognition of group work in occupational therapy is a recent development. Although the importance of constructive activity in maintaining or recovering the health of individuals has been acknowledged for centuries, practitioners and researchers have only recently attempted a systematic approach to the use of group work as a therapeutic tool. In this section we shall examine the various types of groups in use today, the history of the development of group work in occupational therapy, and the current practice in the field. To conclude this section, we shall introduce a model for group work.

1

The Group

Every group develops its own unique character, and yet all groups present to the observer certain common features that enable us to speak of the dynamics of groups. (Benjamin, 1978, p. 6)

Group life has always played an important role in civilization, and throughout history people have considered groups to be essential to survival. We are born into a family group and later expand our social network to include work groups, social groups, recreational groups, and the like. It is through groups that we avoid isolation and learn about ourselves and other people. Many of us participate in group processes even when we are unaware of doing so.

The knowledge we have about groups and how they function is largely the result of social science research that has been conducted over the last 50 years. Studies in the field of group dynamics have led to a clear definition of the characteristics of groups and thus have increased our understanding of a group's potential for bringing about change in organizational behavior, and for achieving therapeutic and educational purposes. In this chapter we shall define the concept of a group and discuss the various characteristics of groups. We shall also briefly describe the properties that make a group therapeutic. Finally, we shall present an overview of four models of group treatment.

Definition of a Group

There are many possible definitions of a group. Mosey (1973) offers the most basic definition: "A group is an aggregate of people who share a common purpose which can be attained only by group members interacting and working together" (p. 45). According to Shaefer, Johnson, and Wherry (1982), "A therapeutic group can be defined as a small, face-to-face group designed to produce behavior change in its members" (p. 2). Mosey's definition is broader and more relevant to this book because it does not exclude groups that may be involved in an activity that precludes meeting face-to-face on an ongoing basis. Loeser (1957) defined a group by describing some of its major characteristics.

1. Dynamic interaction among members. The group process is diminished when most of the action takes place between the individual member and the leader.
2. A common goal. The absence of a common goal diminishes group functioning; a shared, clear goal facilitates group functioning.

3. A dependence on a proper relationship between size and function. When groups are either too large or too small, they cannot function effectively.
4. A dependence on volition and consent. A group functions well only when its members consent freely to be part of that group.
5. A capacity for self-determination. The group functions best in a democratic climate.

We can better grasp these characteristics if we examine a concrete example. Consider a group of people going home from work on a bus. Each of Loeser's characteristics could possibly be applied except for the group's lack of a common goal and self-determination. Even though the riders are aware of other people around them, they are reacting to the bus ride on an individual basis. As long as this is so, they are more accurately called an aggregate or a crowd rather than a group. They would not be called a group until they had an awareness of their dependence on each other to accomplish a goal and an acceptance of the need to interact and meet together to achieve that goal.

Two other qualities of groups are included in Hulda Knowles and Malcolm Knowles' (1959) definition of a group. These are (1) a "group consciousness—the members think of themselves as a group, have a 'collective perception of unity,' a conscious identification with each other" (p. 39), and (2) the "ability to act in a unitary manner—the group can behave as a single organism" (p. 40). These two features characterize a mature group, one that has worked together for some time in order to achieve a certain cohesion.

Social scientists have attempted to classify groups according to common characteristics. Cooley (1909), a sociologist, recognized the special role of the family in the development of young children. He viewed the contacts that occurred within the family as typical of a primary group. A primary group includes close, face-to-face relationships; this type of contact is found in the family, in children's play groups, and in neighborhood groups. The relationships between people in primary groups are characterized by a sense of interdependence and belonging, rather than a sense of individualism. In these groups there is a sense of "we," rather than a sence of "I." Primary groups remain an important source of nurturing and support for adults. Primary group relationships for adults are found in groups of close friends and in small, informal work groups where the emphasis is on closeness, informality, and the satisfaction of personal needs. In contrast to the primary group, the secondary group is characterized by a more formal relationship between members. Secondary groups may also be small, face-to-face groups, but relations are less intimate than in the primary groups. Professional groups, in which people relate more formally through their work roles, are examples of secondary groups. Here the relationships tend to be work- or task-related and entail a more reasoned, less private interpersonal style.

In reality, the distinction between primary and secondary, formal and informal groups is not as clear-cut as in Cooley's description. For instance, although a work group may maintain impersonal and formal relations between workers on the job so that they can get their work done, at the same time the group may be sincerely concerned with the members' feelings about one another. Thus the group combines the features of both primary and secondary groups. The two types of group behavior may be viewed as functions that are present in all groups but in varying proportions. Benne and Sheats (1978) described these functions as (1) group task functions, which enable the group to get its work done and to achieve its goals, and (2) group building and maintenance functions, which contribute to the building of relationships and cohesiveness among group members.

Two features are common to all groups: content and process. The term *content* refers to what is said and discussed during the time that the group meets. It includes both verbal and nonverbal communication. The term *process* refers to the ways in which things are said and in which the work of the group is carried out. This includes how members are relating to one another in the group, who talks to whom, how group decisions are made, and how group tasks are accomplished. These two features appear in every group, be it a meeting of the Board of Directors or a gathering of friends.

These general features or characteristics of a group are common to all groups and appear in various combinations in the numerous definitions of groups presented by social scientists. Beyond these broad features, each group exists as an individual entity and is unlike any other group. As we look closely at different sorts of groups, we shall find various combinations of characteristics that define more precisely the specific groups. The specific characteristics we shall examine are structure, context and climate, composition, cohesion, and stages of development.

Characteristics of Groups

Group Structure

The structure of a group can be defined as the group form, the combination of mutually connected and dependent parts of a group (Howe, 1968). All groups have structure. When we look at group structure, we look at the organization and procedures of the group, considering not only what type of structure the group exhibits but also how much or how little structure is present. These factors will influence the capacity of a group to reach its goals. For instance, when comparing a group that conducts its business according to Robert's Rules of Order with a group that makes decisions through an informal decision-making process, it is easy to see that the two groups exhibit different structures. In the first group, all communication between members is channeled through the chairman and decisions are made by a majority vote. In the second group, all communication occurs directly between members without the intervention of a leader. In the latter case the group may be more spontaneous, but it may also be less efficient. If we look still more closely, we find that although the decision-making process may take a longer time to complete, the results may give members greater satisfaction. Group structure is created from a number of factors, such as the nature of the specific goals of the group, the pattern of leader and member interaction, the composition of membership, the history of the group, and the group climate (Fig. 1-1).

Group Context and Climate

No group exists in a vacuum; rather, it exists in a historical and environmental context. A group may exist because of a historical precedent, and this may be openly stated. A hospital administrator may say, "We've always had an exercise group for our stroke patients." Or a group may be formed in response to a recognized need, such as the need for patients to discuss their plans before leaving the hospital. Still another example of a historical context would be the attitudes that surrounded the formation of a new group. A group that had been the focus of staff controversy in its planning stages may develop an attitude of suspicion toward curious nonmembers. In each of these examples, the historical context is a unique factor influencing the structure of the group. At times the historical context may make it difficult for the group to restate or alter its goals, to

FIG. 1-1. Face-to-face task groups (Circa 1935). (Courtesy of the Boston School of Occupational Therapy Archives, Tufts University, Medford, MA)

broaden or redefine its membership roles, or to refocus the activity of the group. The prestige or attractiveness of the group for its members may also be related to the historical context. A newly organized group is often believed to have a high prestige, thus increasing its attractiveness for present and future members.

In contrast to historical context, which refers to the environment outside the group, the group climate refers to the physical and social environment inside the group. A physical environment that is quiet and attractive, where members are comfortable, is conducive to informal communication. A seating arrangement where members can have face-to-face contact is essential for interpersonal communication. The physical climate is closely related to the social climate. The social climate determines whether members feel accepted, respected, or supported; the climate also determines whether the group can develop a spirit of mutuality between the leader and the members. Ideally, the group climate will be flexible so that the group can adjust to the requirements of the different group tasks.

There is clear evidence that a group can be drawn together through competition with another group. Nevertheless, many researchers question whether the attraction of mutually exclusive rewards, even in the attainment of group goals, is effective in creating an efficient environment for work (Deutsch, 1960). When people undertake a task with an attitude of cooperation and interdependence, there is greater acceptance of ideas, better listening, less possessiveness of ideas, and, in general, better communication. In this type of climate, compared to one that stresses interpersonal competition, the group will strive harder to enhance its achievement and to build a friendlier atmosphere.

10

Group Composition

Size. Group size is related not only to the goals of the group but also to the number of interactions between members. The minimum number for a group is two. Some features of a group of three are not possible in a group of two, such as members forming coalitions. In a small group, membership interaction is restricted and the leader must initiate group action. As more members join the group, the opportunity for people to interact with a variety of individuals increases. If one of the goals of the group is to get feedback and consensual validation for member behavior, the group needs to be large enough to ensure a variety of opinions. Beyond a certain size, the opportunity that each member has to interact with other group members decreases. Frequently, in large groups only the most assertive members of the group are able to express themselves.

The question of group size has been studied extensively by group dynamics researchers. Bales and Borgatta (1962) observed task groups of two to seven members and found that group size influenced the communication patterns. Groups with an even number of members (four or six) had significantly more disagreements and antagonisms and less expression of positive feelings than did groups with an odd number of members (three, five, or seven). Asch (1960) studied small groups and investigated the effect that the size of the majority has on group pressure. He found that a majority of four or more did not produce effects greater than did a smaller majority of three. The main change in group pressure occurred when the majority changed from two to three members. A study by Castore (1962) on the effects of group size on the number of member-to-member interactions in therapy groups found that there was a substantial reduction in the number of interactions when the group size reached nine or more members. Along similar lines, Hare (1962) noted that larger groups tend to produce lower member satisfaction and that as the size of a group increases, the time available for each member to participate decreases.

Open or closed groups. The membership in an open group frequently changes from one group session to the next. There is a continuous turnover in membership as some people leave the group and others join it. In an open group a significant amount of time and effort is devoted to the introduction of new members to the group. Since each group of individuals develops a unique climate, the introduction of new members into the group changes the climate and alters member security. Hare (1962) found in his studies of small groups that the rate of member turnover in open groups influenced the degree of group cohesiveness.

11

Groups in which the membership remains the same throughout the life of the group are called closed groups. Cohesiveness and trust are maximized in a closed group, and thus the potential for learning and behavior change is increased. Yalom (1983) found that this cohesiveness and stable membership are not always constructive. He suggests that over time closed groups might profit from a change in membership. Members in some of the groups he studied stated that the experience of seeing members leave the group increased the pressure on them to do something for themselves. New members also provided old members with an opportunity to help others and to practice social skills with strangers.

The length of time over which a group meets is probably not as important as the total number of hours or sessions. For instance, a group may meet three times a week for 3 weeks, or once a week for 9 weeks. The total number of hours will be the same. The more frequent sessions, however, may increase the intensity of the group experience for the members. In the last few years social scientists have experimented with varying lengths of group time. Marathon groups or extended time sessions over weekends have become popular. Under the pressure of time, the development of the group is accelerated and members undergo a more intense experience. It is not unusual for the length of time that a group meets to be determined by internal factors, such as the time required to complete the chosen task. We often hear of this group as the task force appointed to investigate a specific problem. In other groups, the length may be determined by the time required to meet the group goals. In schools, groups are commonly timed according to external factors such as the length of a semester or a school year.

Voluntary or involuntary membership. Group members come together for many reasons, and the motives of the individual members can affect the success of a group in achieving its goals. Although members may share a common concern, whether or not members joined the group of their own volition can affect the functioning of the group. Involuntary membership may result in apathy or rebellion. The relative attractiveness of members to a group will determine the degree of cohesiveness of that group.

In their research, Cartwright and Zander (1960) identified two factors that attracted members to a group: First, the group itself was viewed as a desirable object, and second, group membership was viewed as a way to satisfy needs that existed outside the group. A group could be deemed attractive either because of the activities available in the group or because of the people who constituted its membership, or both. For instance, a cooking group may be attractive to members because they like to cook and to eat the results of their work. On the other hand, the cooking group may be attractive to members because they want to be with people who are members of that group. The may not be interested in cooking at all. Group behavior is frequently influenced by the degree to which membership in the group is a result of personal choice or compulsion.

Evidence from research suggests that if people are attracted to membership they are more likely to accept the responsibilities of membership (Dion, Miller, and Magnan, 1970). They will also attend the meetings with more regularity (Back, 1951) and persevere in achieving difficult goals (Horwitz, 1960). Members attracted to the group place greater value on the group goals than do members who are not attracted or who are forced to attend (Zander and Havelin, 1960). This research supports the view that benefits are greater from voluntary membership than from involuntary membership. This does not mean that all compulsory membership is unattractive. All people are members of involuntary groups such as the family group, racial groups, and classroom groups. Groups in which membership is not a matter of choice can lead to satisfaction and growth. Lifton (1967) aptly noted that membership in involuntary groups can be a source of security, particularly for dependent individuals.

Group goals. The goals for a group may be specific or general. They may be determined by someone outside the group or by the group itself. How a group is formed and who holds authority for the group may dictate whether goals can be changed and by whom they can be changed. Authorities other than the group leader often specify and regulate the goals of the group. For example, the administrator of a nursing home organizes a group of patients to make decorations for a social event, and the occupational therapy assistant is assigned to lead the group. In this case, the administrator, who is not part of the group, determines the group task and goals, not the group itself or even the group leader.

A group may have more than one goal. Group goals can be a composite of the goals of individual members or a product of the group, the development of the goals representing an effort shared by all members.

There are frequently two levels of goals: personal goals and group goals. While the group is working toward one common goal, members may also be working toward individual goals. When these two levels are compatible, the group will function effectively to reach its goals. When these two levels are incompatible, the goals will need to be reexamined and modified. Similarly, the group leader may have one set of goals and the membership another set of goals. These two sets of goals may be compatible or in conflict with each other. How the various goals are related will influence the achievement of both sets of goals.

Groups fare better when members are clear about their goals. Raven and Rietsema (1957) studied the effect of clarity of goals on the member roles. They found that group members who had a clear understanding of the goals experienced greater feelings of group belongingness and were more involved in the process of achieving those goals. The more time a group spent in working out agreement on clear objectives, the faster it could reach those goals, and the more likely it was that members would reach a consensus. Cartwright and Zander (1960) found that when all members of the group accepted a single goal they became interdependent and were able to improve the quality of group performance through a process of mutual facilitation.

As a group works together to determine its goals, to integrate personal goals into group goals, and to reevaluate the goals and perhaps change them, it increases its productivity. Through work-

13

ing together, group members increase their knowledge of one another and of how they can best work together. Lippitt (1961) outlined four steps that enable a group to increase its productivity.

1. A group should have at the outset a clear understanding of the goals it wants to reach.
2. The group should be aware of its own process. It should continually evaluate that process and make necessary changes.
3. The group should be aware of and understand the skills, talents, and other resources within its membership.
4. The group should create new tasks as needed and terminate those tasks no longer compatible with the goals.

Groups need to choose goals that they can reach within the limitations of their resources. Groups that are realistic about their aspirations tend to be successful in reaching goals, according to Atkinson and Feather (1966). It also seems that when a group is given a set of alternatives, after discussion a group will select a higher risk alternative than will an individual member (Bem et al, 1965).

Leader and membership interaction. The pattern of interaction and communication among all group members can differ from group to group. This interaction can be predominantly verbal, as in group therapy sessions, or mainly physical or active, as in a cooking group preparing a meal. The interactional pattern may be highly structured or informal, spontaneous, and loosely structured. An example of a structured interactional pattern is the high-level in-patient therapy group described by Yalom (1983). In this therapy group, he introduced a structure called an agenda go-round; according to this structure, each member had to formulate a personal agenda for the group session and share his goals for the session with the group. This structure assured that all members would speak up in the meeting and talk about their personal goals in therapy. This can be contrasted with an informal, loosely structured group, in which members may or may not talk as they choose. When they do interact, they choose the context of their own interactions.

The nature of the group goals as well as the type of activity will influence the interactional pattern. Consider a group whose task is to prepare a meal. The planning phase will be mainly verbal. After this phase has been completed members will work individually or in dyads while the meal is being prepared. The group interactional pattern must change if the task is to be completed effectively.

The studies of Lewin, Lippitt, and White (1939) on the impact of different leadership styles on group behavior have shown that leadership influences the group interactional pattern. Under autocratic leadership, the interaction of members was found to be formal and hostile. When the leader assumed a democratic style the interaction patterns of the members were more informal and cooperative. This study will be discussed in more detail in Chapter 5.

A number of different factors influence communication patterns in groups. Festinger and Thibaut (1951) found that between 70% and 90% of the communication in the groups that they studied was addressed to persons whose opinions were at the extremes of the existing range of opinions in that group. Hurwitz, Zander, and Hymovitch (1960) determined that members with "low power" in the group spoke up less and were more conspicuous in their behavior than "high-power" members. Further, low-power members were less liked by both high- and low-power members. In this study the term high-power members referred to persons who had been evaluated as having prestige and the ability to persuade others.

The rules and regulations of membership may also influence the group interactional pattern. Rules may govern attendance, participation, types of acceptable behavior, or the assignment of duties or roles. In some groups, members are not allowed to leave the group before the meeting has ended; in others, they are not allowed to arrive late. It is usually up to the leader to enforce these rules. Sometimes rules are agreed upon by the members and then the group acts as the enforcing body.

The style of the group leader as well as the goals of the group will influence the types of roles that members can assume in the group. These roles may be narrowly prescribed or they may be varied, leaving members free to assume different roles as the need arises. According to Benne and Sheats (1978), roles for group members are of three kinds. First is the "group task role," whose purpose is to assist the group in coordinating its efforts to define and solve common problems. Second is the "group building and maintenance role," which helps the group to function as a group. Members in this role focus on the processes developed to enable everyone to work together as a group and on strengthening or altering those processes as needed. Third is the "individual role," which is concerned solely with the satisfaction of individual needs. Benne and Sheats have described member roles within each of these types.

Twelve roles can be classified as group task roles that assist the work of the group in completing specified task goals.

1. The *initiator—contributor* suggests or proposes new ideas or new ways of viewing the group problems or goals.
2. The *information seeker* asks for clarification of suggestions made, and for authoritative information and facts pertinent to the problem being discussed.
3. The *opinion seeker* asks not primarily for the facts of the case but for clarification of the values pertinent to what the group is doing.
4. The *information giver* offers facts or generalizations that are authoritative, or relates his own experiences to the group problem.
5. The *opinion giver* states a belief or opinion related to a suggestion made or to an alternative suggestion.
6. The *elaborator* makes suggestions in terms of examples and offers a rationale for suggestions made previously.
7. The *coordinator* clarifies the relationships among various ideas and suggestions, tries to pull ideas together, or tries to coordinate the activities of various members or subgroups.
8. The *orienter* defines the position of the group with respect to its goals.
9. The *evaluator—critic* subjects the accomplishments of the group to standards of group functioning in the context of the group task.
10. The *energizer* prods the group into action or decision-making and attempts to stimulate the group to a "greater" or "better" activity.
11. The *procedural technician* facilitates group movement by doing things for the group.
12. The *recorder* makes a record of group suggestions and decisions, or writes down the products of discussion.

Group building and maintenance roles focus on building group processes and attitudes of support and on the maintenance of group-centered behavior. Seven roles fall into this category.

1. The *encourager* praises, agrees with, and accepts the contributions of others. Through these attitudes, he indicates warmth and solidarity toward the other group members.
2. The *harmonizer* mediates differences between members, attempts to reconcile disagreements, and relieves tension in conflict situations.
3. The *compromiser* operates from within a conflict in which his ideas or positions are involved. He may compromise by giving up power, admitting error, or by "coming half-way" in agreeing with the group.
4. The *gatekeeper* or *expediter* attempts to keep communication channels open by encouraging and facilitating the participation of other group members or by regulating the flow of ommunication in the group.
5. The *standard setter* or *ego ideal* expresses standards for the group to achieve in its functioning, or applies norms in evaluating the quality of the group process.
6. The *group observer* or *commentator* keeps records of group process and helps the group to evaluate its own procedures by presenting feedback.
7. The *follower* goes along with the sense of the group, serving as an audience in group discussion.

Individual roles are assumed by individual members of a group to satisfy personal needs that are not relevant to the group task and maintenance functions. When a group experiences a high incidence of "individual-centered" rather than "group-centered" participation, the group should evaluate its functioning.

1. The *aggressor* lowers the status of others, disapproves of the values, acts, and feelings of others, and attacks the whole group or an issue that it is working on.
2. The *blocker* tends to be negativistic, stubborn, disagreeing, and opposing beyond reason.
3. The *recognition seeker* works in various ways to draw attention to himself.
4. The *self-confessor* uses the audience that the group provides to express personal, non-group-oriented communications.
5. The *playboy* displays a lack of involvement in the group's processes.

6. The *dominator* tries to assert personal authority or superiority by manipulating the whole group or selected members of the group. Domination may be in the form of flattery, asserting a superior status, or interrupting the contributions of others.
7. The *help seeker* tries to elicit expressions of sympathy from the group through unreasonable expressions of insecurity or self-deprecation.
8. The *special interest pleader* speaks for special interest groups, usually as a mask for his own prejudices and biases.

The interaction between the leadership and the membership of the group will determine the extent to which members can assume these different roles. Napier and Gershenfeld (1973) list some of the factors that relate to member participation in the group. According to their research, the morale of the entire group will be higher in groups in which members have more access to participation: The more open the participation, the higher the morale. The positions that members take in the group can influence the leadership of the group as well as the potential for conflict among the members.

The pattern of interaction between members and the leader may directly influence the problem-solving and decision-making capacity of the group. It is common for groups to have problems in making a decision. They frequently make a quick decision that fails when the decision is implemented, or they may be unable to reach any decision at all. In both cases, inadequate discussion of the issues involved in the decision may be responsible for the lack of success. The concerns need to be brought out and discussed openly.

Sometimes the nature or obligation of the decision is not clearly understood by the group members, and some changes need to be made. Further, members may have difficulty separating the issues from the members who proposed them. Interpersonal loyalties or conflicts may impinge on the decision-making process and outweigh the importance of the issues themselves.

Probably the most common error in group decision-making is assuming that a vote is representative of the consensus of the group. A vote is often made without the full participation of the group members; leaders of the discussion tend to seek out members who agree with them and avoid those who have no opinion or who disagree. Lippitt (1961) compiled a list of factors that facilitate group decision-making:

1. A clear definition of the problem
2. A clear understanding of who is responsible for the descision
3. Effective communication for producing ideas
4. An appropriate group size for decision-making
5. A means for testing different alternative decisions
6. A commitment to the decision
7. The honest commitment of the leader to the group decision-making process
8. Agreement on the procedures and methods for decision-making before deliberations on the issue

There are no fixed rules for good decision-making, but good leadership can contribute by guiding the group along lines that support member contribution, free expression of opinion, and a unity of purpose.

Group Cohesiveness

The term group cohesiveness appears often in the literature of group dynamics and is one of the goals that groups seek to achieve. There are several definitions of the term group cohesiveness. All refer to the intensity of feeling that members have for the group, to their sense of solidarity, that this is "our group." The term also implies a sense of value about the group, a wish to defend the group against external and internal threats. Frank (1957) refers to this as the attractiveness that the group has for its members. Cartwright and Zander (1960) see cohesiveness as the result of all the forces acting on all the members to persuade them to remain in the group. According to Yalom (1970), " 'Group cohesiveness' is not per se a curative factor but instead a pre-condition for effective therapy. . . . Cohesiveness is both a determinant and effect of intermember acceptance: the members of a highly cohesive therapy group will respond to each other in this manner more frequently than members of a noncohesive group; groups with members who show high mutual understanding and acceptance are, by definition, cohesive" (p. 38).

Some of the elements that contribute to the level of group cohesiveness are the amount of cooperation, caring, and support that exists between members, the encouragement that they show each other, the group attendance rates, and member punctuality at meetings. The degree of trust and risk-taking is also a measure of cohesiveness, as is the amount of group support given to individual members who express their opinions and share their points of view.

Stages of Group Development

Like the individuals who compose them, groups pass through several stages or phases of development during their existence. These phases have been labeled in various ways, according to the behavioral theories held by the observers. In the beginning stages of a group, the members need to get to know each other and to develop a sense of being comfortable in the group. After the group has been meeting for a period of time, members develop ways of interrelating and working together. The path of development is not a straight line, and frequently groups revert to a previous developmental stage when there is a change in structure or when the group is under stress.

Bion (1959), a researcher who contributed extensively to the field of group dynamics from a psychoanalytic point of view, focused on the tensions experienced by group members and on the resolution of these tensions in the process of group development. Group members coped with their tensions in three stages: first, through fighting or fleeing; second, through dependence and counterdependence on the leader; and third, through a process of pairing. Bion concluded that the pairing of the third stage was a way of creating closer bonds between members and thus overcoming the underlying fears and tensions.

William Schutz (1960) presented a theory of group development based on interpersonal needs. He described three stages: inclusion, control, and affection. The inclusion stage involved issues related to belonging or not belonging to the group; the control stage involved issues of dependence and authority; and the affection stage involved issues of intimacy, closeness, and caring.

Bales (1955) and Tuckman (1965) also investigated the dynamics of small groups and described similar stages of group development. Tuckman labeled and outlined four stages.

1. *Forming.* All groups have to deal with the issues of coming together and forming a group. They need to get to know each other, their resources and talents, and their tasks.
2. *Storming.* This is a stage of conflict, disagreement over the task and how it should be completed. Conflicts may also arise over group leadership.

3. *Norming.* By this stage the conflicts have been resolved and the group can develop norms and procedures to carry out its activities. A cohesive unit has begun to form.
4. *Performing.* The group is in control and can work effectively on the task at hand.

According to Tuckman's model of group development, the conflicts of the storming stage are a normal event in group development.

Bennis and Shepard (1956) present yet another theory of group development based on their studies of group dynamics. Before outlining their stages of development, they delineate two major areas of uncertainty for group members: orientation to authority and power, and orientation toward each other. The first phase of this developmental model is concerned with dependence and power relations and includes three subphases. Subphase one, dependence–flight, refers to member behavior designed to please the leader in the hope that the leader will ease the member's anxiety and find a goal and task for him. In trying to be polite, members engaged in "flight" behavior because they discussed matters external to the group. As the leader continued to "fail" the group by not making decisions for the members, expressions of counterdependence replaced dependence and the group progressed to subphase two, counterdependence–fight. In this subphase, expressions of hostility were more frequent and were supported by other members. Subgroups emerged and vied for leadership. This chaos led to a resolution in subphase three, resolution–catharsis. During this phase, the group members assumed leadership roles and the group became unified in its pursuit of a goal. There was pairing and involvement in the group task. The subgroups fused, and the group became ready to move into the second stage.

The second developmental stage of this model relates to group interdependence. Here the group turned its attention to issues of shared responsibility. In subphase four, enchantment–flight, everyone was happy and there was an atmosphere of "sweetness and light." Everyone was amiable and decisions were unanimous, but the decisions made were related to issues about which no one had strong feelings. The harmony of this period soon wore thin and the group again began to form subgroups, leading to subphase five, disenchantment. In this subphase, the group divided into subgroups according to the degree of intimacy required for membership. Again, a resolution of the problem occurred under the pressure of having to accomplish a task. The group now reached the final subphase, consensual validation, which represented an acceptance of the group in realistic terms, with diminishing ties based on a personal orientation. Group consensus became easier to achieve on important issues, and personal ties developed from working together to achieve group goals.

Another group of researchers, Garland, Jones, and Kolodny (1965), who were observers with backgrounds in social group work, described five stages of group development: pre-affiliation, power and control, intimacy, differentiation, and separation. Here again we see the developmental issues to be affiliation, power, intimacy, and interrelatedness or differentiation. The various reports of the research of group observers discussed above show remarkable agreement on the basic developmental issues of small groups.

Curative Aspects of a Group

Up to this point we have talked very generally about groups; in this section we shall turn to the specific aspects of groups that make them therapeutic or conducive to good health. There has been an ongoing controversy between researchers in group dynamics and group therapists regarding the nature of the therapeutic process in a group. Workers in the field of group dynamics tend to make their observations on, and draw their conclusions from, the behavior of the group at the group level. They describe the processes that originate from the group interaction. By contrast, when group therapists observe similar group behavior, they tend to make their observations on the individual level and to see the group processes merely as an example of how individuals relate in a group setting. For group therapists the dynamics that occur in groups are interpersonal dynamics, and therefore no different from those that occur between any two individuals. The controversy between researchers and therapists centers around the question of whether the group process itself has a greater impact on helping a member to change than the efforts of the therapist. A number of researchers have described the therapeutic factors inherent in the group, and a significant overlap and agreement among the studies are apparent (Corey and Corey, 1977; Corsini and Rosenberg, 1955; Yalom, 1975). These researchers noted that the group members described the healing processes as rooted in the interaction between the group members; rarely did the reports recognize a role played by the therapist.

After extensive research, Yalom (1975) identified 11 factors that led to successful group therapy. Again, many of the factors identified in this study were similar to those identified in other studies. Yalom's (1975) 11 curative factors are described below.

Instilling hope. When members are in a group with other people who are in the process of changing, their hopes are reinforced. Members in a group usually function at different points on a health continuum. Hope is nurtured when group members with similar problems appear to profit from their interactions in the group.

Universality. People who seek help in groups often feel that they are alone in their misery and that no one else could be as unacceptable as they feel they are. In the group they learn that others have similar concerns, fears, and experiences. It is reassuring for them to know that they are not truly different from other people even though they may have endured painful experiences in life.

Imparting information. Members learn a great deal about themselves and others through participation in a group. They also learn about the group process itself. Some groups provide extensive didactic information about growth and development or about the treatment of specific diseases or states of dysfunction. Other groups teach actual skills and roles. These skills may be practiced in preparation for discharge to the home or the community.

Altruism. An important aspect of membership in a group is the opportunity to help others and to be helped by others. Members gain a feeling of self-worth when they are able to give to other members and to "make a difference" in others' lives. People need to feel that they are needed. Altruism has traditionally played an important part in the healing rites of primitive cultures.

Corrective recapitulation of the family group. The therapy group is a primary group closely resembling the family group. The leader is often perceived as a parental figure. Past familial experiences influence a member's interaction with other members and with the leader. The therapy group can help a member become aware of, and correct, maladaptive behavior that may have characterized relationships in the family group.

Development of socializing techniques. Socializing techniques, also called social learning or the learning of social skills, vary in importantance and explicitness from group to group. Groups may use learning methods such as role playing and structured exercises to develop specific social skills. An example would be the use of role playing to practice applying for a job or asking someone for a date. For individuals who lack close relationships, the group may be their only opportunity for accurate interpersonal feedback that enables them to learn about another person's reactions to their standard behaviors, such as a lack of eye contact when talking or a display of indifference that may mask feelings of caring. Members in long-term groups learn how to listen, to respond to others, and to be less judgmental about themselves and others.

Imitative behavior. Group members often model their behavior on other members' behaviors. People can learn new behaviors just from watching other people. Additionally, members learn vicariously through the experience of other members who have problems similar to their own. More will be said about modeling as a method of learning in Chapter 5.

Catharsis. The expression and release of feelings is an important part of the healing process in the group. Merely expressing emotion, however, may not be of lasting benefit. Members learn to express feelings and discover that the expression of honest feelings is not as disastrous as may have been feared. It is often a surprise for people to realize that positive and negative feelings toward a person may be present at the same time.

Existential factors. Personal concerns about isolation, death, and helplessness may be discussed and shared in the group setting. For instance, a group of people with a chronic disease may well discuss the limitations impose by the disease, the areas in which they can still exercise choices, and the responsibilities they must assume for those choices. Often, by facing the issues of life and death, life can be lived more honestly; the group lends the support needed to face these issues.

Cohesiveness. Cohesiveness refers to the sense of group belonging and was discussed in an earlier section. Humans are social beings and need to relate to other people. For some people, isolation is a serious problem. Being hospitalized is an isolating experience for most people. The individual is separated from familial support systems, and there are few opportunities to share feelings and to be accepted on a personal level. For hospital patients in particular, the group becomes a place where sharing experiences and feelings can augment the therapeutic aspects of treatment.

Interpersonal learning. The therapy group is a microcosm of society, in which persons interact in much the same way that they would in society or outside the group. By helping each other to understand their behavior within the group, members can get a clearer picture of interpersonal behavior patterns in society at large. Learning in the "here and now" provides individuals with immediate feedback about how others see them. Thus they learn what behavior brings people closer to them or keeps them at a distance, and on the basis of this information they can decide whether to alter their own behavior. This is a process called reality testing.

According to Yalom, most groups include all of the 11 therapeutic factors listed above; different groups emphasize different factors. While the curative factors are to be found within the processes of the group and do not adhere to the role of the leader, we cannot conclude that the style and skills of the leader are of no consequence. Clearly the leader plays an important part in helping the group members establish their interactional pattern and develop norms that assist the group to become cohesive.

Overview of Models of Group Treatment

There are many kinds of treatment groups, conducted in a wide variety of treatment settings, but all can be described under four main categories: activity groups, intrapsychic groups, social systems groups, and growth groups. These types are not mutually exclusive; there is considerable overlap, and some groups may be a combination of two types. Table 1-1 presents an overview of these four models of group treatment. Each group is examined according to four factors: group goals and structure, the theoretical perspective, the role of the leader, and group membership.

Activity Groups

Group goals and structure. Activity groups are small, primary groups in which members are engaged in a common activity or task that is directed toward learning and maintaining occupational performance. According to Fidler (1969), "The intent of the task-oriented group is to provide a shared working experience wherein the relationship between feeling, thinking and behavior, their impact on

TABLE 1-1.
OVERVIEW OF MODELS OF GROUP TREATMENT

Type of Group	Group Goal	Theoretical Perspective	Leader Role	Membership
Activity group	Related to the acquisition and maintenance of occupational performance: 1) task 2) role	The role of purposeful activity ("doing") in maintaining and developing skills changes in small groups (Mosey, 1981; Fidler, 1969)	1) to create a group climate that facilitates interaction 2) to provide support 3) to structure the level of group activity	1) heterogeneous or homogeneous 2) select members according to level of skill development
Intrapsychic group	To achieve personality change through: 1) insight 2) tension reduction 3) transference	Psychoanalytic theory and activity group therapy (Slavson, 1950)	1) to explore and interpret personal member conflicts 2) to analyze free association and transference	Requirements: 1) intact ego 2) ability to think abstractly 3) homogeneous or balanced heterogeneous group
Systems group	To focus on the how of group behavior in the present	Systems theory as applied to group dynamics; Lewin (1951) life space and interaction theory of human behavior	1) to participate as an expert member 2) to establish appropriate group climate for process analysis	1) varies from group to group 2) shared goal and views within the group
Growth group	1) to increase member sensitivity to self and to others 2) to learn through action-oriented experiences	Existential and humanistic concepts, such as in Schutz (1967); Rogers (1961); Perls (1971); and Maslow (1962)	1) to facilitate group interaction 2) to model behavior	A self-selected homogeneous group desiring increased awareness and personal growth

26

others and on task accomplishment and productivity can be viewed and explored. . . . Task accomplishment is not the purpose of the group but hopefully the means by which purpose is realized. It is seen as the catalytic agent which elicits behavior and interaction, brings into focus both functional capacities and limitations, facilitates collaboration in working through problems and provides a concrete reality factor against which to measure learning and achievement" (p. 45).

Although the goals and activities of task-oriented groups may differ, these groups have inherent structures and goals of therapeutic value for the members. The activity group, with its focus on function relating to the task at hand, closely replicates living in the community or the family. In this climate, with a concrete activity on which to focus the group's attention and an opportunity for learning from direct experience, group members learn more easily and with increased understanding.

The given task provides a degree of form and organization that is helpful to many group members. When the activity goals are clear, the skills and roles necessary to meet these goals become evident, and the involvement and comfort of members increase. Members are given the opportunity to coordinate and use the skills that are available within the group. In this way people can work on that part of the task in which they have greater skill. For example, a person who is shy or who has poorly developed verbal skills may become involved in the group primarily through joining in the task itself. On the other hand, a member who is afraid of the physical demands of the task or who cannot get involved because of physical limitations can participate on the verbal level. Learning occurs in the shared process of "doing" as well as through the process of discussion. In the process of "doing," all available skills become important for the completion of the task and members are drawn together in joining their skills toward accomplishing a single goal. The activity also provides a concrete measure of the progress of the group as a whole toward the achievement of the group tasks and goals. Through their individual contributions, the members may also clearly demonstrate their growth and achievement over time.

The given task of the acitivity group may serve the needs of the members in different ways. In some cases, group members may feel more comfortable working on a task than on interpersonal relationships. These members identify with the group through their involvement in the task activity. Other members may be comfortable in the group setting but have difficulty dealing with the nonhuman environment; they need the opportunity to learn how to solve specific problems through participation in a joint activity. For these members, accomplishing the task may be the major goal. For all members, a sense of belonging and partnership can result from the exploration of a shared need to master the nonhuman environment.

Mosey (1981) describes six major types of activity groups. These types are not meant to be discrete, since some groups may have the properties of several categories; the description of types is meant to clarify and facilitate communication.

1. *Evaluation groups:* Designed to assess an individual's areas of function and dysfunction within a group setting, thus evaluating both interpersonal and activity skills. The role of the therapist is primarily that of an observer, and the activity is chosen by the therapist.
2. *Task-oriented groups:* Designed to increase members' awareness of themselves and others in the activity process and in their interactions with other members. The role of the therapist or leader is to help members explore the relationships between thoughts, feelings, and actions.
3. *Developmental groups:* Designed to teach only group interaction skills, based on the theory that group interaction skills are developmentally stage-specific. The role of the therapist varies with the developmental level of the group.
4. *Thematic groups:* Designed to help members learn the knowledge, skills, and attitudes necessary for accomplishing a specific set of activities.
5. *Topical groups:* Same goals as those of the thematic groups except that these goals are carried out independently in the community. One type of topical group, the anticipatory group, focuses on activities that the group members anticipate doing in the future. A second type of topical group, the concurrent group, focuses on activities that the group members are currently doing in the community. In this group, the therapist helps group members share experiences, give each other feedback, and offer suggestions.
6. *Instrumental groups:* Designed to assist members to maintain their level of function and to meet health needs. Change, although it may occur, is not expected. The role of the leader is to select activities that meet the goals described above.

Although the groups that Mosey describes as activity groups are generally considered occupational therapy groups, activity groups also include social work groups, such as those following the Vinter model (Galinsky and Schopler, 1974) and some groups in the field of nursing (Sampson and Marthas, 1977).

Theoretical perspective. The concept supporting the activity group has its roots in two different theoretical constructs: The first is the principle of group dynamics relating to how the curative factors in small groups bring about positive behavioral change; the second relates to the importance of "doing"—the role of purposeful activity in maintaining and developing skills.

Leader role. The role of the leader in the activity group would vary according to the particular group's goals. The leader's responsibilities generally include (1) creating a group climate that facilitates interaction of group members, provides support for members, and relates group processes to the concerns of the members; (2) selecting appropriate activities or helping the group to do so; (3) structuring the activities for the group's level; (4) acting as a role model; and (5) guiding the learning of interpersonal and task skills. In most cases, the group is dependent on the leader to select and structure the task, particularly in the early stages of the group.

Group membership. In selecting group members, a prospective member's cognitive, social, emotional, and perceptual-sensory skills need to be considered. In addition, one must consider the ability of the members to function in the spheres of work, play, and self-care. Depending on the goals of the particular group, a leader may select members who are similar or different in age, sex, sociocultural background, educational level, and identified problem areas.

Intrapsychic Groups

Group goals and structure. The general aim of intrapsychic groups is to achieve characterological and personality changes in each group member by "working through" the personal, intrapsychic, and historical antecedents of the present maladaptive personality patterns. The term intrapsychic refers to the processes and conflicts that occur within the individual. Insight into the unconscious and the self is the goal of psychoanalytic therapy. In addition to insight, groups can offer activity experiences that meet group needs and provide ego support for the members (Howe, 1968). Groups of this type include psychoanalytic therapy groups, projective occupational therapy groups, art therapy groups, and psychodrama groups.

Theoretical perspective. Intrapsychic groups are primarily based on psychoanalytic theory. The principles of psychoanalytic therapy are applied to the group setting, with the focus of observation and analysis placed primarily on the individual member, not on the group. Transference is a phenomenon that has particular importance in the intrapsychic group. In projective occupational therapy groups and art therapy groups, object relations theory, including human and nonhuman objects, is also useful. In activity group therapy as developed by Slavson (1950) members work out their intrapsychic, preconscious conflicts through activities, and therapeutic results are obtained more through the discharge of tension inherent in the conflict than through insight.

Leader role. In these groups the leader primarily guides members in their exploration, interpretation, and "working through" of personal conflicts. In addition, the leader may help individual members by validating and clarifying their perceptions of reality. Leader techniques include encouraging free association and analysis of transference. To encourage member participation, the leader might make available projective media, such as clay, paints, paper, or music. The group members are dependent on the leader for the analysis and interpretation of their behavior.

Group membership. Members must have a clear ego identity and cognitive ability in order to use the group to develop insight; that is, they should be able to deal in the realm of the abstract. In these groups membership is usually homogeneous in age, sex, and socioeconomic status. Groups are carefully structured for a balance of problem areas and characterological style.

Social Systems Groups

Group goals and structure. The general aim of these groups is to help participants learn about group processes and dynamics through participation in a collective task experience. "Our attention is directed to how relationships within groups are formed and how these relationships stabilize; how decisions are made; how patterns of behavior emerge; how parts fit together to form the whole family, team, or group" (Sampson and Marthas, 1981, p. 125). Groups of this type include T-groups, laboratory methods groups, and other educational group laboratories.

Theoretical perspective.   The principles behind social systems groups are drawn from systems theory and are applied to the concepts of group process and group dynamics. Kurt Lewin (1951) is frequently identified as the founder of this theoretical perspective. He described the behavior of individuals in terms of a system of paths, barriers, forces, and goals. He coined the term *life space*, which refers to the environment experienced by the individual or the group. A group has a life space, in that it operates in a milieu within which it plans activities and conducts its business. Lewin focused on the here-and-now activity of the group and the interaction with its environment at the present time.

Leader role.   The role of the leader is to participate in the group as a member—expert and to establish an environment appropriate for process analysis. The leader tries to keep member attention focused on the "how" rather than the "why," or on here-and-now events rather than on intrapsychic issues in the group's exploration of its processes relative to the task that it seeks to accomplish. The members' dependence on the leader is situational and transient.

Group membership.   Since social systems groups are educational in nature and do not focus on individual member concerns, the membership varies. Despite changing membership there may be a single focus, concern, or goal for the group so that members can maintain the group.

Growth Groups

Group goals and structure.   Growth groups are generally aimed at increasing members' sensitivity to feelings or enhancing members' ability to help themselves through the power of the group. The precise methods by which these goals are accomplished vary from group to group, but all are aimed at personal growth through didactic and action-oriented experiences. According to Shaffer and Galinsky (1974), "The Encounter format offers an intensive group experience that is designed to put the normally alienated individual into closer contact — or 'encounter' — with himself, with others, and with the world of nature and pure sensation" (p. 211). Groups included in this category are encounter groups, sensitivity training groups, and marathon groups. Self-help groups belong in this category too, but they differ in that they are frequently conducted as leaderless groups.

Theoretical perspective. Growth groups are based on the principles of humanistic and existential philosophy and psychology that seek to fulfill the potential inherent in each person. These principles are explained in the writing of such leaders as Carl Rogers (1961), William Schutz (1967), Fritz Perls (1971), and Abraham Maslow (1962).

Leader role. The role of the leader in growth groups is to facilitate interaction, learning, and experience among the group members. The leader often teaches through a modeling process — for example, by modeling openness, spontaneity, the expression of feelings, and mutual aid. The group members are dependent on the leader only as a teacher or contributor to the group. Frequently the leader is seen only as the person who initially organized the group.

Group membership. Members are individuals who seek a growth experience and will therefore share a desire for growth. Most likely members will range in age from adolescence to older adulthood.

Conclusion

A wide variety of groups are available to meet the therapeutic and educational needs of individuals. The types of groups listed in this chapter do not exhaust the list of possibilities. Groups can be designed to suit any particular need or goal. Research has shown the types of interactions that group leaders can expect and has also indicated appropriate responses and techniques for dealing with these interactions.

References

Asch, S. E. (1960). Effects of group pressure upon the modification and distortion of judgments. In D. Cartwright and A. Zander (eds.), Group Dynamics: Research and Theory. Evanston, IL: Row, Peterson.

Atkinson, J. W., and Feather, N. (1966). A Theory of Achievement Motivation. New York: John Wiley & Sons.

Back, K. (1951). Influence through social communication. Journal of Abnormal Psychology 46: 9–23.

Bales, R. F. (1955). Adaptive and integrative changes as sources of strain in social systems. In A. P. Hare, E. F. Borgatta, and R. F. Bales (eds.), Small Groups. New York: Knopf.

Bales, R. F. (1955). The equilibrium problem in small groups. In A. P. Hare, E. F. Borgatta, and R. F. Bales (eds.), Small Groups. New York: Knopf.

Bales, R. F., and Borgatta, E. F. (1962). Size of group as a factor in the interaction profile. In A. P. Hare, E. F. Borgatta, and R. F. Bales (eds.), Small Groups (2nd ed.). New York: Knopf.

Bem, D., Wallach, M., and Kogan, N. (1965). Group decision making under risk of aversive consequences. Journal of Personal and Social Psychology 1: 453–460.

Benjamin, A. (1978). Behavior in Small Groups. Boston: Houghton Mifflin.

Benne, K., and Sheats, P. (1978). Functional roles of groups members. In L. Bradford (ed.), Group Development (2nd ed.). La Jolla, CA: University Associates.

Bennis, W. B., and Shepard, H. S. (1956). A theory of group development. Human Relations 9: 415–457.

Bion, W. R. (1959). Experiences in Groups. New York: Basic Books.

Cartwright, D., and Zander, A. (1960). Group Dynamics: Research and Theory (2nd ed.). New York: Harper & Row.

Castore, G. F. (1962). Number of verbal interrelationships as a determinant of group size. Journal of Abnormal Social Psychology 64: 456–457.

Cooley, C. H. (1909). Social Organization: A Study of the Larger Mind. New York: Scribner's.

Corey, G., and Corey, M. S. (1977). Groups: Process and Practice (2nd ed.). Monterey, CA: Brooks/Cole.

Corsini, R., and Rosenberg, B. (1955). Mechanisms of group psychotherapy: Process and dynamics. Journal of Abnormal and Social Psychology 15: 406–411.

Deutsch, M. (1960). The effects of cooperation and competition upon group

33

process. In D. Cartwright and A. Zander (eds.), Group Dynamics: Research and Theory (2nd ed.). New York: Harper & Row.

Dion, K. L., Miller, N., and Magnan, M. (1970). Cohesiveness and social responsibility as determinants of group risk taking. Proceedings of the Annual Convention of the American Psychological Association 5 (Part I): 335–336.

Festinger, L., and Thibaut, J. (1951). Interpersonal communication in small groups. Journal of Abnormal and Social Psychology 16: 92–99.

Fidler, G. (1969). The task-oriented group as a context for treatment. American Journal of Occupational Therapy 23: 43–48.

Frank, J. D. (1957). Some determinants, manifestations, and effects of cohesiveness in therapy groups. International Journal of Group Psychotherapy 7: 53–63.

Galinsky, M. J., and Schopler, J. H. (1974). The social work group. In J. B. Shaffer and M. D. Galinsky (eds.), Models of Group Therapy and Sensitivity Training. Englewood Cliffs, NJ: Prentice-Hall.

Garland, J. A., Jones, H. E., and Kolodny, R. (1965). A model for stages of development in social work groups. In S. Bernstein (ed.), Explorations in Group Work. Boston: Boston University School of Social Work.

Hare, A. P. (1962). Handbook of Small Group Research. New York: Free Press of Glencoe.

Horwitz, M. (1960). The recall of interrupted group tasks: An experimental study of individual motivation in relation to group study. In D. Cartwright and A. Zander (eds.), Group Dynamics: Research and Theory (2nd ed.). New York: Harper & Row.

Howe, M. (1968). An occupational therapy activity group. American Journal of Occupational Therapy 22: 176–179.

Howe, M. (1968). A Review of Selected Professional Literature Describing Four Youth Groups to Determine Structure with Reference to Psychiatric Occupational Therapy. Unpublished master's thesis, San Jose State University.

Hurwitz, J. I., Zander, A., and Hymovitch, B. (1960). Some effects of power on the relations among group members. In D. Cartwright and A. Zander (eds.), Group Dynamics: Research and Theory (2nd ed.). New York: Harper & Row.

Knowles, M., and Knowles, H. (1959). Introduction to Group Dynamics. New York: Association Press.

Lewin, K. (1951). Field Theory in Social Science. New York: Harper & Row.

Lewin, K., Lippitt, R., and White, R. (1939). Patterns of aggressive behavior in experimentally created social climates. Journal of Social Psychology 10: 271–299.

Lifton, W. M. (1961). Working with Groups: Group Process and Individual Growth (2nd ed.). New York: John Wiley & Sons.

Lippitt, G. L. (1961). How to get results from a group. In L. P. Bradford (ed.), Group Development. Washington, D.C.: National Training Laboratories, National Education Association.

Loeser, L. H. (1957). Some aspects of group dynamics. International Journal of Group Psychotherapy 7 (1): 5–19.

Maslow, A. (1962). Toward a Psychology of Being. Princeton: Van Nostrand.

Mosey, A. C. (1973). Activities Therapy. New York: Raven Press.

Mosey, A. C. (1981). Occupational Therapy: Configuration of a Profession. New York: Raven Press.

Napier, R., and Gershenfeld, M. K. (1973). Groups: Theory and Experience. Boston: Houghton Mifflin.

Perls, F., Hefferline, R. E., and Goodman, P. (1971). Gestalt Therapy. New York: Bantam.

Raven, B. H., and Rietsema, J. (1957). The effects of varied clarity of group goal and group path upon the individual and his relation to his group. Human Relations 10: 29–44.

Rogers, C. (1961). On Becoming a Person. Boston: Houghton Mifflin.

Sagi, P., Olmstead, D., and Atlesk, F. (1955). Predicting maintenance of membership in small groups. Journal of Abnormal Social Psychology 51: 308–331.

Sampson, E., and Marthas, M. (1981). Group Process for the Health Professions (2nd ed.). New York: John Wiley & Sons.

Schutz, W. C. (1960). FIRO: A Three-Dimensional Theory of Interpersonal Behavior. New York: Rinehart, Wilson.

Schutz, W. C. (1967). Joy: Expanding Human Awareness. New York: Grove Press.

Shaefer, C., Johnson, L., and Wherry, J. (1982). Group Therapies for Children and Youth. San Francisco: Jossey-Bass.

Shaffer, J. B., and Galinsky, M. D. (1974). Models of Group Therapy and Sensitivity Training. Englewood Cliffs, NJ: Prentice-Hall.

Slavson, S. R. (1950). Analytic Group Psychotherapy with Children, Adolescents, and Adults. New York: Columbia University Press.

Tuckman, B. W. (1965). Developmental sequence in small groups. Psychological Bulletin 63: 384–399.

Yalom, I. D. (1970). The Theory and Practice of Group Psychotherapy. New York: Basic Books.

Yalom, I. D. (1975). The Theory and Practice of Group Psychotherapy (2nd ed.). New York: Basic Books.

Yalom, I. D. (1983). Inpatient Group Psychotherapy. New York: Basic Books.

Zander, A., and Havelin, A. (1960). Social comparison and intergroup attraction. Human Relations 13: 21–32.

35

2

History of Occupational Therapy Group Treatment

Occupational therapists have been using groups in their treatment plans since the 1920s, and today the group can be found as a treatment tool in all areas of occupational therapy. As the use of group treatment increased in all specialties of occupational therapy during the 20th century, the role of the occupational therapist and the nature of the group as a treatment tool changed. In Chapter 1 we examined several different types of groups. The state of current practice will be addressed in Chapter 3, and in Chapter 4 we shall present a model of the functional approach to group work. In this chapter we shall examine the history of group work in occupational therapy, investigating the trends and forces leading to the occupational therapy group as it is known today.

The history of group work in occupational therapy falls into five periods or eras: (1) project era, (2) socialization era, (3) group dynamics—process era, (4) ego building—psychodynamic era, and (5) adaptation era. As we explore the development of groups as a treatment tool, we should keep in mind the following questions:

1. How did occupational therapy evolve over time?
2. What forces led to the shift, in occupational therapy, from an individualized to a collective approach?
3. How did group treatment contribute to the development of occupational therapy?
4. How does group treatment fit into the occupational therapy profession as a whole?

Although the history of group work as an acknowledged tool of occupational therapists does not officially begin until 1922, when Adolph Meyer (1922/1977) described the use of individual craft projects in a group setting, the use of group work as a tool for healing already had a long if unappreciated history in Western civilization. Asclepiades, who was born more than 100 years before Christ, was the first physician to recommend activity as a treatment for patients with mental illness. He advised physicians to treat patients *"safely, quickly, pleasantly"* (Licht, 1948, p. 1). Occupational therapy was thus practiced long before it was given its "20th century name," to use Bockoven's (1971) expression. Kielhofner and Burke (1977) also note that "the use of occupation as a form of treatment for the physically or mentally ill is documented throughout recorded history" (p. 678).

The moral treatment movement of the 19th century is cited most often as the immediate historical origin of occupational

FIG. 2-1. A singing group. (Courtesy of the Boston School of Occupational Therapy Archives, Tufts University, Medford, MA)

therapy (Bing, 1981; Bockoven, 1971; Gillette and Kielhofner, 1979; Kielhofner and Burke, 1977). The moral treatment movement itself emerged from the humanitarian trends of the 18th and 19th centuries (Gillette and Kielhofner, 1979; Kielhofner and Burke, 1977). The objective of this movement was to correct attitudes and habits of living. "The physical, temporal, and social environment was *engineered* so as to correct *faculty* [*sic*] *habits of living* and regenerate new ones. . . . It employed the moral remedies of education, daily habits, work, and play as therapeutic processes for normalizing disorganized behavior in the mentally ill" (Kielhofner and Burke, 1977, p. 678). The patients' programs apparently included individual and collective activities. The group activities seem to have been orchestrated solely by the therapist. In describing an aspect of his program in Paris in 1840, Leuret presented group activity as it might have appeared to the casual observer:

> To some I assign reading out loud, reading verses or singing. Reading is usually performed by several patients who recite alternate passages or sentences from a story according to a plan which I have devised. . . . Some do not enter into this exercise with much cooperation, but pray or grumble instead.

But as he continues his description, he touches on goals and achievements that are still sought by therapists today.

> Once they overcome their initial distaste, stimulated by the example of others and by the presence of an audience, they begin to apply themselves to the work which they eventually accept with pleasure. Those who read well, drill others and soon their self-esteem improves and they become better teachers than I could ever be. (Leuret, 1840/1948, p. 64)

The goals and procedures Leuret used are remarkably similar to those used by occupational therapists today. He apparently structured the activity and group processes according to what is now called a developmental continuum. The proponents of the 19th century moral treatment movement thus strongly influenced the practice of early 20th century pioneers in occupational therapy by serving as models.

The Project Era, 1922-1936

It is difficult to identify when and by whom the first occupational therapy groups were conducted. Perhaps the confusion stems from the large number of definitions of group treatment or from the failure of therapists to identify their practice as group treatment. Most likely the first occupational therapy groups were groups of patients working on individual activities in a clinic or on a ward. They were probably an organized unit but not necessarily a group with a unified goal or interdependent task. This sort of unit can be called a collective, whereas a unit with a unified goal or interdependent task is more strictly defined as a group. The collective offers a setting that is most like individual therapy, and the group provides a setting with a strong sense of group centeredness.

The nature of the collective unit, as opposed to the group, dominates the years between 1922 and 1936 and gives rise to the name of this period. During these early years the focus of the members in a collective was on individual projects, which were completed in the open setting of the collective (Fig. 2-2). There was little or no emphasis on the process of interaction taking place among the members of the collective while they worked on their individual projects in the company of others.

During the early years of the 20th century, there was enough interest in this sort of activity to lead therapists to found a

FIG. 2-2. (A,B) Occupational therapy collectives. (Courtesy of the Boston School of Occupational Therapy Archives, Tufts University, Medford, MA)

professional organization. Thus, in 1917, the National Society for the Promotion of Occupational Therapy was founded (Reed and Sanderson, 1980). Five years later, in 1922, the first official journal of occupational therapy was published. In the first issue of the *Archives of Occupational Therapy*, Adolph Meyer and Eleanor Clarke Slagle individually described occupational therapy collectives. Meyer (1922/1977) observed,

> It had long been interesting to see how groups of a few excited patients can be seated in a corner in a small circle of two or three settees and kept wonderfully contented picking the hair of mattresses, or doing simple tasks not too readily arousing the desire for big movements and uncontrollable excitement and yet not too taxing to their patience. Groups of patients with raffia and basket work, or with various kinds of handwork and weaving and bookbinding and metal and leather work, took the place of the bored wall flowers and of mischiefmakers. (p. 640)

43

In a similar vein, Slagle (1922) suggested a program that included collectives. Slagle advised moving the patient through a series of four steps. The steps progressed from individual habit training, to the "kindergarten group" for "stimulating the special senses," to occupational therapy ward classes focusing on the individual, and, finally, to the "occupational center," or "curative workshop," for helping the patient adapt to other members of the group (pp. 15–16). In the final phase, the patient was moved from supervised activity to a collective focusing on vocational goals. Slagle called this the preindustrial group (p. 16).

Both Meyer and Slagle viewed the activities in collectives as a means for patients to develop socially acceptable habits to replace their pathological reactions. Thus the Project Era begins with a formalization of the philosophy of 19th century moral treatment. This formalization, however, was only one thread from the previous century influencing 20th century professionals.

During the last decades of the 19th century, historically named the Progressive Era, America was becoming a scientific and industrialized society (Wiebe, 1967). There was an increase in scientific concerns, developments in technology, booming industrialism, increased urbanization and immigration, and a shift from shop to factory in industry (Wiebe, 1967). Women were fighting for the right to work in an occupation of their choice (Smuts, 1959). According to Wiebe (1967), these changes called for a new set of values and a new kind of social order.

Like many other institutions, hospitals changed during this period, and these changes had a crucial impact on the developing health professions. Rosner (1979) points out that because of the economic and social forces of the depression of the 1890s, hospitals changed from charity institutions to paying institutions: "The move away from charity to pay services was rationalized as part of the larger Progressive Era movements toward order, efficiency and bureaucracy" (Rosner, 1979, pp. 118–119). By 1922, when Meyer and Slagle described occupational therapy, these forces had already had an effect. Patients now did part of the labor of the institution. Activities necessary for the daily operation of the hospital, such as farming, laundry, and sewing, were called occupational therapy (Rothman, 1980).

As early as 1923, a therapist surmised that there was an economic rationale for prescribing work as occupational therapy. Canton (1923) stated,

> It is interesting to note that work originally was given only to state patients, planned to relieve employees rather than to effect cures, and managed from the viewpoint of utility. It was found that other patients wished to share in these employments and since the relatives who were paying for their care sanctioned the arrangement, they too, were permitted to putter around so that now the proper use of time in some helpful and gratifying activity has become a fundamental issue in the treatment of all neuro-psychiatric patients. (Canton, 1923, p. 348)

The occupational therapy collective thus became an economic unit, in which the patient was also a worker.

The recognition of a connection between activity and health could have led to several results, not only to the collectives in which members worked on projects or on minor jobs for the institution in which they lived. Yet the path through this development is reasonably clear and direct. If we look more closely at the founders and early practitioners in this field, we can perhaps understand the choice of emphasizing collective or group work over jobs or products.

When the National Society for the Promotion of Occupational Therapy was formed in 1917, its membership included medical doctors, social workers, teachers, nurses, and artists (Hopkins, 1978). Most of the members were women, and this was in character with the times. "The proportion of all women workers who were professionals grew from 11.9 per cent in 1920 to 14.2 per cent in 1930" (Chafe, 1972, pp. 89–90). Occupational therapy thus began as a female-dominated profession. These founding women were likely to be from upper class families and to be familiar with handicrafts and family or group living. They were also probably quite comfortable directing groups of people in a collective milieu. The role of women in founding and defining occupational therapy is sometimes neglected in historical analyses, leading to the false conclusion that occupational therapy is more like the male-dominated professions in health care. In fact, the women in occupational therapy shaped the direction that the field took in this early era, choosing collective work because of their background.

There was no mention of groups in the occupational therapy literature from 1923 to 1936, but in 1936, 14 years after Meyer's and Slagle's papers were first published, an interest in groups reappeared. Three papers on occupational therapy group treatment were published in 1936. In these articles there is evidence that therapists were beginning to conceive of the gathering of patients as a group rather than only as a collective. Further, therapists were now dividing responsibility for a single project among several patients and viewing opportunities for involvement in a project as a device for restoring health.

Although the role of occupational therapy was not specified, L. Cody Marsh (1936) advocated that relatives of psychotic patients be given group treatment. Davis and Dunton, in 1936, as mentioned by Gleave (1947), described a form of mass occupational therapy in which patients had the opportunity to associate with a group project and to increase their self-respect through the group's accomplishment. In an attempt to improve the use of group activity, Anderson (1936) suggested "project work," or "individualized group therapy." In project work, the therapist structures the activity to meet the group member's individual needs while still requiring each member to contribute to a larger group project.

Anderson emphasized that project work should not be confused with the activity usually offered by occupational therapy departments:

> Project work, with its designated therapeutic aims and offered for its therapeutic values, must not be confused with that type of group activity often provided in many institutions as a part of "hospital economy," "doing odd jobs," time filling activity, or furnishing labor needs of the institution with no reference to the value of the work for the individual concerned. Nor is project work the same as occupational therapy where the

guest usually works in a group or alone on an individual project but not with the responsibility of contributing a part to a project which is the divided responsibility of an entire group. (Anderson, 1936, p. 265)

This is the first clear indication that the type of group work should be defined according to the patient, and not according to the hospital and its economic needs or according to the physician's or therapist's interests.

Anderson clearly departed from the norm when he suggested occupational therapy should focus on the patients' therapeutic needs, rather than fulfill the institution's labor needs. Nevertheless, he emphasized that the therapist was responsible for carrying out the doctors' "therapeutic aims" and should regularly report to them. These "therapeutic aims," using Anderson's terms, were to "provide an outlet for aggressions," "permit propitiation of guilt," "provide freedom for fantasy expression," and "permit opportunity to create" (p. 265).

The reports and advances by Anderson and others came after more than a decade of silence. Why did it take so long for group treatment to be mentioned again in the occupational therapy literature? Why was the process of development a slow one? The following writers may give us some answers to these questions.

In her historical analysis of the development of occupational therapy, Woodside (1971) pointed out that in the years between 1910 and 1929 occupational therapy developed into an active and organized profession. The first set of minimal educational standards were published in 1923; occupational therapy schools became affiliated with colleges and universities in the 1920s; and occupational therapists were first required in 1929 to be registered with a specific set of credentials. According to Rerek (1971), the profession defined its direction in the mid-1930s by asking the American Medical Association to establish standards for occupational therapy education and to accredit each new school. This, Rerek assumed, was when the profession formally assumed a medical ancillary role. Between the years 1922 and 1936, therefore, the focus of the profession was on the development of occupational therapy as a profession.

The climate of the mid-1930s stimulated professionals to reconsider the form of occupational therapy group treatment. During the depression many occupational therapy departments closed, decreased their personnel, or struggled with limited supplies (Reed and Sanderson, 1980; Rerek, 1971). By this time, the field of medicine had professionalized and had increased its interest in scientific pursuits (Markowitz and Rosner, 1979). In addition, the harsh realities of the depression meant fewer women could enter male-dominated careers (Chafe, 1972). The limited number of jobs that did exist were given to men, as the primary wage-earners in a household. More and more women turned to those areas of the economy that were traditionally open to them. This led to an increase in the number of aspiring professional women in services related to other professions. Thus women, with training in handicrafts and group techniques, filled the ranks of the occupational therapy profession and continued to shape the field throughout the 1930s.

It should not be surprising, then, that Rothman (1980) found that in the 1930s "the most popular and prevalent form of hospital 'treatment' throughout these years remained occupational therapy" (p. 344). According to Rothman, "for most inmates, occupational therapy involved daily assignments to endless chores, chores as meaningless to their lives as they were important to the survival of the institution" (Rothman, 1980, p. 346). Patients were not yet free from an economic role. Jobs were selected because they were necessary for the maintenance of the institution, not because of any specific interests or treatment goals for the patients. Rothman (1980) emphasized that "occupational therapy . . . was more than an occasional patient weaving or joining the wheelbarrow brigade. As in correctional institutions, it affected the very existence of the mental hospital, for inmate labor was essential to day-to-day maintenance of the facility" (p. 346).

Occupational therapy group treatment was clearly a development of the times. Hospitals established to treat patients also needed patient labor. The strong interest of women in the profession shaped the content and structure of that labor. Since women were taught many crafts as part of their upbringing, they were perhaps most able to teach inexpensive craft activities to groups of dependents as well as to supervise group tasks of maintenance. Canton (1923) noted earlier in occupational therapy the aide must be both a teacher and a nurse. "She will be the kind of person who needs the little touches which would make even the most barren place a bit homelike, and a certain amount of buzzing activity which is part of every normal environment. . . . In addition she must bring to the work the ability to teach certain projects now accepted as valuable occupations" (Canton, 1923, p. 355). Finally, the willingness of female therapists to conduct group treatment under male supervision left the usually male

47

FIG. 2-3. A project group. (Courtesy of the Boston School of Occupational Therapy Archives, Tufts University, Medford, MA)

physician more time to pursue his new scientific and professional interests. As these elements combined to shape the outer form of the profession, researchers in the field were laying the groundwork for changes in the internal form of treatment.

Anderson (1936) was probably the first to identify a structure for occupational therapy groups that would change behavior. In his view, the group is seen as a curative tool rather than as a way to keep patients occupied. In Anderson's project group, the elements of activity and group process foster personality change (Fig. 2-3). Anderson pointed out that group activities can fulfill ordinary health needs as well as therapeutic aims:

> In project work the guest actively participates as a member of a group in work, provided as far as practicable out of doors, which is of value to the entire group. Therapeutic aims, which may be to provide an outlet for aggressions, permit propitiation of guilt, provide freedom for fantasy expression, permit opportunity to create, and others designated by the psychiatrist in charge of the guest are followed for each individual and this permits and makes necessary individualization of the work within the larger group. In addition to the therapeutic values

determined upon a psychiatric basis, this out-of-door activity
has the additional advantage of being physical exercise per-
formed in the open air and sunshine. (p. 265)

Anderson's new vision of group therapy brought to an end the formative era that had called attention to the economic as well as to the
therapeutic value of treating patients in groups. By the end of The
Project Era, the occupational therapy group was a recognized tool
for achieving prescribed therapeutic aims.

The Socialization Era, 1937–1953

From 1937 to 1953, the literature on occupational therapy continued
to grow. During this period the purpose of groups changed from
individual activities to an environment providing opportunities for
socialization among psychiatric patients. Groups afforded patients an
outlet for social needs and a vehicle for experiencing the gratification
that comes from positive social contact. This period of group history
is therefore called the Socialization Era.

In 1937 Dunton described quilt-making as a group activity
that aided socialization. Three years later, Blackman (1940) supported
the use of a literary club for the group treatment of schizophrenics
(Fig. 2-4). The club's purpose was to work out "social cravings." In
1947 two publications described groups for socialization purposes.
Lockerbie and Stevenson (1947) noted that group activities and clubs
are valuable for socialization problems found in psychiatric hospitals.
Basing her work on Slavson's group therapy approach, G. Margaret
Gleave (1947), an occupational therapist, suggested the use of group
therapy with children to provide a permissive, socializing atmosphere.

Slavson has been called the father of group psychotherapy
(Schiffer, 1979); he also had a major influence on group treatment
in occupational therapy, and his ideas were especially influential
during this period. In 1934 Slavson designed his first group treatment
method for children (Schiffer, 1979), based upon the group work he
conducted from 1911 to 1930. According to Schiffer, "these [Slav-
son's] earlier groups were concerned primarily with the personal
enrichment of individuals through active participation in creative
pursuits" (p. xiii). In about 1934, Slavson drew important conclusions
about the curative effects of creative activities in a peer group environment. Schiffer (1979) reported what Slavson told him in an
interview at the time:

FIG. 2-4. A literary club. (Courtesy of the Boston School of Occupational Therapy Archives, Tufts University, Medford, MA)

> He finally confirmed his original premise: it was the element of *compresence*, the actuality of being and interacting one with the other in the peer group, the sense of self-worth gained from newly acquired skills, the self-selected, completed craft and art projects, fortified by the spontaneous praise of fellow members, and the improved social status that were responsible for the corrective effects on personality and character. (pp. xvi–xvii)

It is likely that occupational therapists followed Slavson's lead in their use of activity groups for socialization purposes during the 1940s. Let us now examine the work of therapists during this period.

Hyde, York, and Wood (1948) viewed games as an effective means for improving the socialization of psychiatric patients in a mental hospital (Fig. 2-5). White (1953) discussed the use of simplified repetitive activities that can include large groups of patients and can be structured for maximum involvement. Koven and Shuff (1953) found that guided group activity, such as gardening, painting, and museum trips, promotes cooperation, social awareness, and a sense of gratification through group achievement.

Taking a somewhat different approach, Halle and Landy (1948) recommended the integration of group activities, such as craft and art activities used in occupational therapy, with group psychotherapy. They found that the subject matter in the art activities group often correlated with the subjects being discussed by the psychiatrist in group psychotherapy. In 1947, Solomon and Fentress described the use of "dramatized psychodynamics" in analytically oriented group psychotherapy. The authors discussed the technique of dramatization of psychodynamics but not its use in, or relationship to, occupational therapy groups.

51

The techniques for groups described above were developed and implemented during the Depression of the 1930s and during World War II and its aftermath. These historic events account in large part for the growing trend of using groups to treat large numbers of patients. The severe budget cuts of the 1930s (Rerek, 1971) were followed by an increased demand for therapists during World War II (Jantzen, 1972). With the increasing demand for therapists trained in the techniques of occupational therapy group treatment, the profession was forced to expand its training programs. During World War II, 13 occupational therapy education programs were founded in association with established colleges or universities (Jantzen, 1972). Before World War II, there were only 5 educational programs; 3 were in independent proprietary schools, 1 was in a hospital, and only 1 was in an undergraduate liberal arts college (Jantzen, 1972). The 1940s brought new programs in this field to the forefront of educational growth.

The 1940s meant tremendous growth in occupational therapy, despite budget cuts. Groups enabled a therapist to treat large numbers of patients within a limited time. Because there was still relatively little theoretical orientation, occupational therapists remained in need of supervision and continued to serve an ancillary role. As an extension of the physician, the therapist could treat many patients at a lower cost while continuing to provide necessary medical treatment. The close relation between medicine and occupational therapy no doubt explains why physicians dominated the articles in this field. Of nine occupational therapy journal papers published on occupational therapy group treatment during this period, four were published by male physicians, three were co-authored by a male

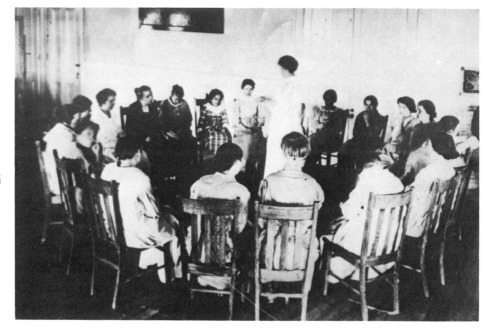

FIG. 2-5. Group games. (Courtesy of the Boston School of Occupational Therapy Archives, Tufts University, Medford, MA)

physician and a female occupational therapist, and only two were authored by female occupational therapists.

The Group Dynamics–Process Era, 1954–1961

The 1950s brought a shift in occupational therapy group treatment. Professionals now recognized the group's curative powers and sought to use them to achieve therapeutic goals. In addition, therapists or leaders were structuring their role and the group's membership and activities to meet a variety of patients' needs. Therapists no longer assumed that all patients in group treatment have the same needs.

These changes resulted in part from two factors. First, occupational therapists were now exposed in their training to the concept of group dynamics. Therapists learned how to manipulate a group in order to achieve specific therapeutic aims. They learned that the group could be used as an environment to produce change in, or support for, specific kinds of behavior. This was indeed an era of group dynamics and process. Second, the introduction of somatic therapies, particularly drugs, enabled patients to function more easily in social settings, freeing the therapist of the earlier concern for socialization and maintenance (Feuss and Maltby, 1959). Therapists could now concentrate on treating specific problems of individual patients and on developing new forms of the group to meet those needs.

In 1954 Fidler and Fidler proposed ways in which groups could be used to facilitate treatment and suggested a new concept of occupational therapy as a laboratory for experimentation of behavior. This concept and its model differed from previous models because Fidler and Fidler recognized the curative effects of the learning, practicing, and modeling of healthy interpersonal behaviors that occurred naturally in an occupational therapy group. Recognizing the limitations of verbal groups for helping chronic psychotic patients, Bobis, Harrison, and Traub (1955) observed the progress of patients in an occupational therapy activity group: "Group projects were emphasized with patients working together or doing different parts of a project. Suggestion was used a great deal by the occupational therapist—steady, gentle urging to participate in the group or group project" (p. 20). They found that patients showed a higher adjustment level in the activity group setting; the authors concluded that the group played an important role in the patients' improvement. Activity group therapy seemed to be the more effective method for chronic, nonverbal psychotic patients.

Nelson, Mackenthun, Bloesch, Milan, Unrein, and Hill (1956) developed groups for differing types of patients, diagnoses, goals, and objectives. They structured "group occupational therapy" for, among others, insulin patients, postlobotomy patients, and male geriatric patients. A graded group program was designed especially for women. Patients were selected for one of three groups according to their level of adjustment. The group members were homogeneous in their level of ability, rather than in their diagnoses, in order to enable them to benefit from socialization opportunities in a particular group structure. The occupational therapist's role ranged from a passive participant in the higher level group to the active encourager who meets needs and structures activity in the lower level group. Combs (1959) designed activities for a custodial care group of elderly men in a chronic disease hospital, structuring them so that the patients moved from activities primarily concerned with individual performance to ones concerned with group performance.

In 1958, an experimental sheltered workshop program was implemented in a home for the aged. Because the authors believed that "for the group as a whole, work for which one is paid is worthwhile activity" (Lakin and Dray, 1958, p. 173), wage earning activity was structured into a group situation as a therapeutic modality. There were several positive effects for the group, including maintenance of adequate self-image and increased social contact.

Springfield and Tullis (1958) conducted a pilot study to determine a method for resocializing chronic patients. The average period of continuous hospitalization for these patients was 31 years, and all subjects were characteristically apathetic. The researchers found improvement was more noticeable in the activity group than during times when the project was not being conducted. Springfield and Tullis noted, "We were fully aware that if our program was to succeed, the emphasis must be placed on interpersonal relations rather than on any special activity" (p. 248).

Moss and Stewart (1959) developed a program for geriatric patients in order to facilitate movement from hospital to community. They developed groups for particular patient needs. "The patients were divided into treatment groups according to their specific disabilities or needs" (p. 268). For example, one group of patients with organic disorders was given training in self-care activities, while a group of confused and withdrawn patients was given simple individual tasks that these patients could successfully complete, since they needed motivation and reassurance. After several months in generalized activities, the therapist suggested that the patients work on one group project. In a similar project, the therapist chose eight men who could benefit from intensive group activity. The group worked on one large project rather than on smaller individual projects related to a common goal.

The 1950s were also a period of increased theoretical research and publishing. The American Occupational Therapy Association conducted an institute on the theme of "interpersonal relationships" (AOTA, 1955). Topics such as "Diagnosing Factors in Interpersonal Relationships," "Developing Effective Patterns of Leadership," and "Understanding the Complexities of Staff Relationships" were discussed. Types of leadership, functions of leadership, group dynamics and factors, and group processes were included. The proceedings of the institute were published for the association membership in the *American Journal of Occupational Therapy*. Similarly, Gibb (1958) wrote on general group process principles for occupational therapists. He described how to make groups more effective using concepts of group dynamics as guiding principles. The 1956 Allenberry Workshop held a conference on the function and preparation of the psychiatric occupational therapist, and the proceedings were edited by Wilma West (1959). Participants made recommendations for the education of the occupational therapist in the use of group techniques, for the psychodynamics of interpersonal relationships in a group, for group dynamics, for use of the therapist as a therapeutic tool, and for selection of group activities. There was discussion of the function of the psychiatric occupational therapist. It should not be surprising that in the 1950s "the majority of [occupational therapy] schools felt that teaching group relations is of major and vital importance . . . that their students need both theory and practice in groups" (West, 1959, p. 173).

By the early 1960s papers on group treatment were emphasizing the importance of the interpersonal relationship between the occupational therapist and patient, and the role of activity in fostering patient adjustment (Fidler and Fidler, 1960; Gratke and Lux, 1960; Novick, 1961). This practice also received empirical support. In 1959, Efron, Marks, and Hall actually compared the benefits to schizophrenic patients of an individual-centered activity (called traditional occupational therapy) and a group-centered activity (making lawn chairs for the hospital). They found no significant difference in benefits between the activities. They found, "however, there is some support for the hypothesis that, for the activities studied, the personality of the therapist is more important than the activity per se" (p. 123/555). Like earlier studies of occupational therapy group treatment, this investigation was not conducted by occupational therapists but by three male therapists in a Veterans Administration Hospital (a Ph.D., M.D., and Ed.M.).

The increase in the use of group treatment in the 1950s resulted from several factors. After World War II many veterans were in need of psychiatric treatment to help them readjust to peacetime. With the availability of medication to control behavior, therapists could design groups to help patients move from hospital life to community living (Feuss and Maltby, 1959; Moss and Stewart, 1959). It is not coincidental that occupational therapists, many of whom were employed by the army, applied concepts from the growing field of group dynamics to their practice. Another factor was the interest of social scientists in studying small group behavior (Mosey, 1971). Four major studies on the use of occupational therapy group treatment for community adjustment of psychotic patients were conducted in Veterans Administration Hospitals during the 1950s (Bobis, Harrison, and Traub, 1955; Efron, Marks, and Hall, 1959; Levine, Marks, and Hall, 1957; Nelson et al., 1956).

The changes that occurred in this period stem from occupational therapists' more sophisticated understanding of specific diseases, the development of psychiatric theories that viewed problematic interpersonal relationships as the cause of mental illness, the use of a team approach and medication in the care of psychiatric patients, and the new theoretical perspective of social scientists who were studying small groups (Mosey, 1971). Moreover, many therapists in the 1950s were more prepared to apply theoretical material to their practice, a result of several schools' standards that required them to complete an undergraduate degree before admission into an occupational therapy certificate program (Jantzen, 1972).

The Ego Building–Psychodynamic Era, 1962–1969

By the end of the 1950s, occupational therapy, like other life sciences, had shifted its focus from a holistic to a reductionist paradigm (Kielhofner and Burke, 1977). This shift resulted from medicine's attempt to achieve scientific status by becoming more like physical science and its subsequent pressuring of occupational therapy to accept a reductionist model as well (Kielhofner and Burke, 1977).

The emphasis on group dynamics and process in occupational therapy group treatment was different from the technical view of patients and treatment emerging in the 1950s. However, the growth of reductionism in other areas of occupational therapy and in medicine was more influential than the trend toward more holistic occupational therapy group approaches. With the growth of a holistic perspective in group treatment, one may wonder if occupational therapists who led groups were different from their professional counterparts who did not lead groups. Regardless, given the historically subordinate position of all occupational therapists, this scenario was predictable. According to Kielhofner and Burke (1977), "by the end of the 1950s, the reductionist model was brought into occupational therapy as the basis of a new paradigm" (p. 682). The reductionist paradigm, they observed, took three forms: (1) the kinesiological model, (2) the psychoanalytic, or interpersonal communication, model, and (3) the sensory integrative, or neurological, model. The three models reflected the attempt to establish a scientific basis for practice.

These forms of a single paradigm are termed reductionist because of the single goal they share. Therapists attempted to define more narrowly the specific goals to be achieved and to achieve them in a more direct manner. Therapists attempted to help patients explore the intrapsychic determinants, or psychodynamics, of their maladaptive behavior through a task-oriented group. The occupational therapy group was often aimed at developing ego strengths: the patient's ability to test reality, apply judgment, make decisions, and modify behavior on the basis of self-observation. The growth of the 1950s was now strictly channeled to achieve specific ends.

The 1960s was also an era of change in many other areas. Diasio (1971) summarized crises having major social impact: the Vietnam War, urban riots, planned obsolescence, campus unrest, rising crime, inflation, and environmental pollution. Balanced against these crises were the more positive trends of the consumer protection movements, peace and civil rights movements, women's liberation movements, concern for the ecology and community health programs, the desire for community control, and the human potential movement (Diasio, 1971). These social crises and movements in turn affected group treatment. Like other professionals, occupational therapists perceived the need for social and scientific accountability.

Research in this period reflects the growing awareness of the need for long-term concern. In their dynamic "four-phase concept" approach, Linn, Weinroth, and Shamah (1962) suggested that the occupational therapist provide an "unstructured work situation" so that changes in the patient's psychiatric illness could be detected. They, two physicians and an occupational therapist, hypothesized that the patient hospitalized for an acute psychiatric illness progressed through four distinct phases: (1) acute emotional decompensation, (2) initial emotional restitution, (3) predischarge symptom flare-up, and (4) meaning reaction (following discharge from inpatient treatment). This concept of group treatment followed trends in hospital psychiatry.

Fidler (1966) described the prototype for occupational therapy group treatment in the psychodynamic era of the 1960s. She stated, "These groups are structured for the purpose of providing a group experience wherein members may explore the many and varied problems which arise in the process of task selection and completion such as decision making, accepting responsibility, being productive and sharing with others. Individual feelings and behavior are discussed in terms of how they impede or enhance group cohesiveness and task accomplishment" (p. 73). This approach supported the concept of milieu therapy. Material brought up in occupational therapy groups was then discussed in verbal psychotherapy and other individual and group therapies.

As the research described above indicates, occupational therapy groups were guided by two fundamental principles during the Psychodynamic Period. First, if exposed to a healthy milieu of accepting and cooperative staff and a variety of self-initiated activities with a range of emotional–interpersonal demands, the patient will develop or reconstitute ego skills necessary for community living (Barker and Muir, 1969; Fidler and Fidler, 1963; German, 1964; Lamb, 1967; Llorens, 1968; Llorens and Johnson, 1966; Llorens and Rubin, 1967; Reilly, 1966; Shannon and Snortum, 1965; Slavson, 1967/1979). Second, if given an interpersonal task in a group, opportunity for the group to develop into a cohesive unit, feedback on the nature of interactions, and modeling of appropriate social skills or responses, the patient can develop ego skills for adapting to interpersonal situations (Fidler, 1966, 1969; Gillette and Mayer, 1968; Howe, 1968; Johnston, 1965; Mosey, 1968, 1969; Owen and Newman, 1965; Rothaus, Hanson, and Cleveland, 1966; Shannon and Snortum, 1965). Thus, through occupational therapy groups, individuals found healthy modes of self-expression, gained improved self-esteem, and found emotional satisfaction of their needs. The goals and methods of occupational therapy groups thus became in part like those of psychotherapy groups.

The 1960s were a hallmark period for occupational therapy group treatment. Many papers describing occupational therapy group formats were written during this period, and group work flourished as a form of treatment. The concern for a scientific approach was exemplified by the many empirical papers on occupational therapy group treatment. Several of these studies focused on the effectiveness of activity groups for promoting social interaction (Ellsworth and Colman, 1969; Gralewicz, Hill, and Mackinson, 1968; Pasework and Hornby, 1968; Pearman and Newman, 1968; Werner, Maddigan, and Watson, 1969). The American Occupational Therapy Association responded to its membership's need for a more sophisticated understanding of evaluation methods, treatment planning, and treatment of psychiatric patients (Mazer, 1968). In an attempt to encourage participation in the newly developing community mental health programs and to improve professional training in the treatment of psychiatric patients, the Association conducted national and regional educational institutes from 1964 through 1968. These seminars supported the psychiatrists' dynamic model of group psychotherapy and adapted it to occupational therapy by introducing an activity process into the group (Gillette and Mayer, 1968). Once again, occupational therapists responded to the external pressures of the medical community as well as to the growing social concerns and needs of the general public.

The Adaptation Era, 1970–Present

The reductionist trend of the 1960s did not last beyond the decade and ultimately left many occupational therapists dissatisfied with their roles as therapists. Kielhofner and Burke (1977) speculated that in the 1960s occupational therapists were concerned with the inadequacy of their theoretical knowledge and were confused about their roles as health professionals. The two researchers surmised, "The problems of social adaptation, for which the medical model was inadequate and which was not addressed by reductionism, are anomalies that earmarked the failure of reductionism in the clinical arena of occupational therapy" (p. 685).

The advances of medical research in developing drugs to treat a wide range of mental illnesses and in expanding our understanding of biological and chemical processes did not resolve the problems of living in the world for people coping with life day to day. As more types of patients were defined, the limits of medicine, strictly defined, came to be recognized. Medical treatment could not aid the chronically disabled, nonverbal, or noninsightful to cope with living among other people. As practitioners in the field of occupational therapy came to recognize the types of problems still unsolved, they sought forms of group therapy that would address these problems. Thus, in the 1970s and 1980s the literature on occupational therapy groups focused on problems of adaptation. The groups described in papers are designed to help patients meet their health needs, cope with skill deficiencies, overcome performance problems, and manage environmental constraints.

The newly developing goals and concerns of the profession were reinforced by external economic factors. During the 1970s the

U.S. economy faced a severe recession, which led to restricted funding, reduced hospital stays, increased demand for quality assurance, and improved cost-benefit ratios. Along with the demands for more efficient and economical services, occupational therapy faced an extensive shortage of trained personnel between 1970 and 1981. The Bureau of Labor Statistics of the United States Department of Labor predicted a "substantial shortfall of occupational therapy personnel" through 1990 (Acquaviva and Presseller, 1983, p. 79). According to Acquaviva and Presseller (1983), "over the past 15 to 20 years we have seen rapid growth in supply of personnel, with a concurrent rapid expansion of the demand for occupational therapy services, resulting in an overall shortage of personnel. That shortage has become more acute in the late 1970s and early '80s at a time when our ability to satisfy that shortage is diminishing. The ramifications of this situation are very serious" (pp. 79–80).

Group treatment flourished in the economic climate of the 1970s. Given the need for serving large numbers of patients, at a reduced or maintained cost, with fewer personnel, the need for occupational therapy group treatment will probably continue to grow in the 1980s. The number of occupational therapists enrolled in an accredited entry-level masters program has increased dramatically. For example, in 1970 142 students were enrolled in such programs; by 1981, 577 students were enrolled ("Dataline," 1982). These students are being trained in the use of groups as a treatment modality. Many of them will probably view group treatment as a preferred tool in their careers as practitioners, or promote and implement group programs in their careers as administrators.

Regardless of the type of education they received, occupational therapists have been educationally prepared to work with groups since the early 1970s (Delworth, 1972; "Essentials of an Accredited Educational Program for the Occupational Therapist," 1975; "Essentials of an Approved Educational Program for the Occupational Therapy Assistant," 1976; Maynard and Pedro, 1971; Posthuma and Posthuma, 1972). The importance of group dynamics, self-awareness, and the interdisciplinary team has also been stressed in occupational therapy curricula and practice (Odhner, 1970b; Steiner, 1972). The educational trends of the 1970s are now being followed by an increased use of groups in the 1980s.

The direction of the theoretical work of the present period was signaled by Ellsworth and Colman (1969), who proposed that treatment be based on behavior principles, specifically, the behavioral approach of B. F. Skinner. This theoretical approach allowed therapists to concentrate on helping patients adapt their behavior to situational needs and goals. Occupational therapy groups in this period have focused on the patients' skill deficits (Denton, 1982; Fidler, 1984; Goldstein, Gershaw, and Spraflin, 1979; Herson and Luber, 1977; Hughes and Mullins, 1981; Kramer and Beidel, 1982; Maslen, 1982; Mosey, 1970a, 1970b, 1981; Neistadt and Marques, 1984; Stein, 1982; Talbot, 1983) and social well-being (Mosey, 1973a, 1973b, 1974). Whether the group is for treatment of a physical problem or an emotional one, the emphasis seems to be on social adaptation through structured, graded learning experiences.

Occupational therapy groups of the Adaptation Era are generally based on one of three factors: (1) diagnosis, (2) role, or (3) setting. Groups based on diagnosis include hemiplegic exercise groups (Bouchard, 1972) or stroke groups (Wilson, 1979), emotion groups (Angel, 1981), groups for hyperactive and learning disabled children (Cermak, Stein, and Abelson, 1973; McKibbin and King, 1983), spinal cord injury groups (Mann, Godfrey, and Dowd, 1973), alcoholism groups (Lindsay, 1983), groups for regressed and elderly psychiatric patients (Noce, Breuninger, and Noce, 1983; Ross and Burdick, 1978), schizophrenics (King, 1974; Linn, Caffey, Klett, Hogarty, and Lamb, 1979; Odhner, 1970a; VanderRoest and Clements, 1983), and borderline patients (Goodman, 1983), arthritis range of motion ("ROM") groups, and many more. Groups focusing on roles deal with the physically disabled (Versluys, 1980), women (Donohue, 1982), elderly and adolescent psychiatric patients (Mahier and Tachabrun, 1978), children with emotional disorders (Fahl, 1970), psychiatric patients in the community (Broekema, Danz, and Schloemer, 1975; Heine, 1975; Webb, 1973), as well as groups for occupational therapy students (Botkins, 1979) and occupational therapists returning to the job market (Labovitz, 1978). Groups concerned with the setting include groups for acute care facilities (Corry, Sebastian, and Mosey, 1974; Neville, 1980), psychiatric out-patient clinics (Kuenstler, 1976), extended care facilities (Fearing, 1978), community elderly (Menks, Sittles, Weaver, and Yanow, 1979), geriatric day hospitals (Aronson, 1976; Kiernat, 1976), and emergency psychiatric settings (Hyman and Metzker, 1970). The unifying thread in these groups is their concern for helping the patient develop daily living skills and function through adaptation.

The group approach to treatment has become the most economical for both the patient and the service delivery system.

Increased hospital costs and the movement of patients into community programs have necessitated a behavioral, skills-oriented learning approach, and this has quickly become the paradigm for occupational therapy groups.

Conclusion

The adaptation approach of the 1970s and 1980s echoes the introduction of occupational therapy groups in the 1920s; in fact there are many reports of activity-focused groups in the Adaptation Era (Falk-Kessler and Froschauer, 1978; Fearing, 1978; Goldstein and Collins, 1982; Kiernat, 1979; Rance and Price, 1973; Rider and Gramlin, 1980; Schwartzberg, Howe, and McDermott, 1982; Shuman, Marcus, and Nesse, 1973). But these contemporary groups are only superficially like the early groups in 1922. Today there is clearly a functional aim and a theoretical rationale for the group, as well as the use of a self-expressive media, an activity of daily living, and a craft.

In the Project Era, the early form of the occupational therapy group was described as a collective. This was an organized unit, although it did not necessarily have a unified goal or an interdependent task like the group-centered unit. By the 1970s, the Adaptation Era, the group format was determined according to specific factors related to the patients, as well as the type of reimbursement and staffing available. Today, patients' skill deficits, degrees of social well-being, diagnoses, and role problems are considered when forming groups in an occupational therapy program. Finally, the conceptual model and theoretical orientation are now regularly considered in choosing the format of a group. For example, in a long-term program with a behavioral orientation, patients with minimal self-care skills are often placed in a parallel, didactic skills learning group similar to the collective. For higher functioning patients in an acute care program with a bio-psycho-social orientation, occupational therapy might take a more interdependent group approach and stress self-awareness through group self-expression activities.

The occupational therapist of the 1980s is also different from the therapist of the Project Era. Although women have dominated this profession throughout its history, the definition of the therapist has changed. Women have moved into the mainstream of work in America and have demanded more formal higher education.

As a result, occupational therapists are now better educated and are drawn from more varied socioeconomic backgrounds.

Even as its form has changed through the years, professionals remain convinced of the value of the occupational therapy group as a treatment tool. Occupational therapy groups have provided service to many patients, often in times of severe economic crisis in America. This explains in part why they have been so important to therapists, patients, and physicians. During the next few decades, we can expect a deeper understanding of the curative as well as rehabilitative effects of occupational therapy group treatment, and a growing interest in its use.

63

References

Acquaviva, F. A., and Presseller, S. (1983). Nationally speaking: Occupational therapy manpower. American Journal of Occupational Therapy 37(2): 79–81.

American Occupational Therapy Association (1955). Institute: Theme interpersonal relationships. American Journal of Occupational Therapy 9(5): (Part II) 212–223, 230–232.

Anderson, C. L. (1936). Project work—An individualized group therapy. Occupational Therapy and Rehabilitation 15(4): 265–269.

Angel, S. L. (1981). The emotion identification group. American Journal of Occupational Therapy 35(4): 256–262.

Aronson, R. (1976). The role of an occupational therapist in a geriatric day hospital setting—Maimonides Day Hospital. American Journal of Occupational Therapy 30(5): 290–292.

Barker, P., and Muir, A. M. (1969). The role of occupational therapy in a children's inpatient psychiatric unit. American Journal of Occupational Therapy, 23(5): 431–436.

Bing, R. K. (1981). Eleanor Clarke Slagle Lectureship—1981. Occupational therapy revisited: A paraphrastic journey. American Journal of Occupational Therapy 35(8): 499–518.

Blackman, N. (1940). Experiences with a literary club in the group treatment of schizophrenia. Occupational Therapy and Rehabilitation 19(5): 293–303.

Bobis, B. R., Harrison, R. M., and Traub, L. (1955). Activity group therapy. American Journal of Occupational Therapy 9(1): 19–21, 50.

Bockoven, J. S. (1971). Occupational therapy—A historic perspective. Legacy of moral treatment—1800s to 1910. American Journal of Occupational Therapy 25(5): 223–225.

Botkins, S. (1979). A peer discussion group of senior occupational therapy students. American Journal of Occupational Therapy 33(2): 123–125.

Bouchard, V. C. (1972). Hemiplegic exercise and discussion group. American Journal of Occupational Therapy 26(7): 330–331.

Broekema, M. C., Danz, K. H., and Schloemer, C. U. (1975). Occupational therapy in a community aftercare program. American Journal of Occupational Therapy 29(1): 22–27.

Canton, E. L. (1923). Psychology of occupational therapy. Archives of Occupational Therapy 2(5): 347–357.

Cermak, S. A., Stein, F., and Abelson, C. (1973). Hyperactive children and an activity group therapy model. American Journal of Occupational Therapy 26(6): 311–315.

Chafe, W. H. (1972). The American Woman: Her Changing Social, Economic, and Political Roles, 1920–1970. New York: Oxford University Press.

Combs, M. H. (1959). An activities program in a custodial care group. American Journal of Occupational Therapy 13(1): 5–8, 26–27.

Corry, S., Sebastian, V., and Mosey, A. C. (1974). Acute short-term treatment in psychiatry. American Journal of Occupational Therapy 28(7): 401–406.

Dataline (1982). Occupational Therapy Newspaper 36(11): 3.

Delworth, U. M. (1972). Interpersonal skill development for occupational therapy students. American Journal of Occupational Therapy 26(1): 27–29.

Denton, P. L. (1982). Teaching interpersonal skills with videotape. Occupational Therapy in Mental Health: A Journal of Psychosocial Practice and Research 2(4): 17–33.

Diasio, K. (1971). Occupational therapy—A historical perspective: The modern era—1960 to 1970. American Journal of Occupational Therapy 25(5): 237–242.

Donohue, M. V. (1982). Designing activities to develop a women's identification group. Occupational Therapy in Mental Health: A Journal of Psychosocial Practice and Research 2(1): 1–19.

Dunton, W. R. (1937). Quilt making as a socializing measure. Occupational Therapy and Rehabilitation 16(4): 275–278.

Efron, H. Y., Marks, H. K., and Hall, R. (1959). A comparison of group-centered and individual-centered activity programs. Archives of General Psychiatry 1(5): 120/552–123/555.

Ellsworth, P. D., and Colman, A. D. (1969). A model program: The application of operant conditioning principles to work group experience. American Journal of Occupational Therapy 23(6): 495–501.

Essentials of an accredited educational program for the occupational therapist (1975). Established and adopted by the American Occupational Therapy Association, Inc. Council on Education October 1972 in collaboration with the American Medical Association Council on Medical Education. Adopted by the American Medical Association House of Delegates, June 1973. American Journal of Occupational Therapy 29(8): 485–496.

Essentials of an approved educational program for the occupational therapy assistant (1976). Established and adopted by the American Occupational Therapy Association, Inc., April 1975. American Journal of Occupational Therapy 30(4): 245–263.

Fahl, M. A. (1970). Emotionally disturbed children: Effects of cooperative and competitive activity on peer interaction. American Journal of Occupational Therapy 24(1): 31–33.

Falk-Kessler, J., and Froschauer, K. H. (1978). The soap opera: A dynamic group approach for psychiatric patients. American Journal of Occupational Therapy 32(5): 317–319.

Fearing, V. G. (1978). An authors group for extended care patients. American Journal of Occupational Therapy 32(8): 526–527.

Feuss, C. D., and Maltby, J. W. (1959). Occupational therapy in the community. American Journal of Occupational Therapy 13(1): 9–10, 25.

Fidler, G. S. (1966). A second look at work as a primary force in rehabilitation and treatment. American Journal of Occupational Therapy 20(2): 72–74.

Fidler, G. S. (1969). The task-oriented group as a context for treatment. American Journal of Occupational Therapy 23(1): 43–48.

Fidler, G. S. (1984). Design of Rehabilitation Services in Psychiatric Hospital Settings. Laurel, MD: Ramsco.

Fidler, G. S., and Fidler, J. W. (1954). Introduction to Psychiatric Occupational Therapy. New York: MacMillan.

Fidler, G. S., and Fidler, J. W. (1960). Introduction to Psychiatric Occupational Therapy (2nd ed.). New York: MacMillan.

Fidler, G. S., and Fidler, J. W. (1963). Occupational Therapy: A Communication Process in Psychiatry. New York: MacMillan.

German, S. A. (1964). A group approach to rehabilitation occupational therapy in a psychiatric setting. American Journal of Occupational Therapy 18(5): 209–214.

Gibb, J. R. (1958). The occupational therapist works with groups. American Journal of Occupational Therapy 12(4): 205–214.

Gillette, N. P., and Mayer, P. R. (1968). The group method in occupational therapy. In J. L. Mazer (Project Director), Final Report Rehabilitation Services Administration Grant #123-T-68 for Field

Consultant in Psychiatric Rehabilitation. New York: American Occupational Therapy Association.

Gillette, N., and Kielhofner, G. (1979). The impact of specialization on the professionalization and survival of occupational therapy. American Journal of Occupational Therapy 33(1): 20–28.

Gleave, G. M. (1947). Occupational therapy in children's hospitals and pediatric services. In H. S. Willard and C. S. Spackman (eds.), Principles of Occupational Therapy. Philadelphia: J. B. Lippincott.

Goldstein, A. P., Gershaw, N. J., and Spraflin, R. P. (1979). Structured learning therapy: Development and evaluation. American Journal of Occupational Therapy 33(10): 635–639.

Goldstein, N., and Collins, T. (1982). Making videotapes: An activity for hospitalized adolescents. American Journal of Occupational Therapy 36(8): 530–533.

Goodman, G. B. (1983). Occupational therapy treatment: Interventions with borderline patients. Occupational Therapy in Mental Health: A Journal of Psychosocial Practice and Research 3(3): 19–31.

Gralewicz, A., Hill, B., and Mackinson, M. (1968). Restoration therapy: An approach to group therapy for the chronically ill. American Journal of Occupation Therapy 22(4): 294–299.

Gratke, B. E., and Lux, P. A. (1960). Psychiatric occupational therapy in a milieu setting. American Journal of Occupational Therapy 14(1): 13–16.

Halle, L., and Landy, A. (1948). The integration of group activity and group therapy. Occupational Therapy and Rehabilitation 27(4): 286–298.

Heine, D. B. (1975). Daily living group: Focus on transition from hospital to community. American Journal of Occupational Therapy 29(10): 628–630.

Hersen, M., and Luber, R. F. (1977). Use of group psychotherapy in a partial hospitalization service: The remediation of basic skill deficits. International Journal of Group Psychotherapy 27(3): 361–376.

Hopkins, H. L. (1978). An historical perspective on occupational therapy. In H. L. Hopkins and H. D. Smith (eds.), Willard and Spackman's Occupational Therapy (5th ed.). Philadelphia: J. B. Lippincott.

Howe, M. C. (1968). An occupational therapy activity group. American Journal of Occupational Therapy 22(3): 176–179.

Hughes, P. L., and Mullins, L. (1981). Acute Psychiatric Care: An Occupational Therapy Guide to Exercises in Daily Living Skills. Thorofare, NJ: Charles B. Slack.

Hyde, R. W., York, R., and Wood, A. C. (1948). Effectiveness of games in a mental hospital. Occupational Therapy and Rehabilitation 27(4): 304–308.

Hyman, M., and Metzker, J. R. (1970). Occupational therapy in an emergency psychiatric setting. American Journal of Occupational Therapy 24(4): 280–283.

Jantzen, A. C. (1972). Some characteristics of female occupational therapists, 1970. Part III: A comparison: Faculty and clinical practitioners. American Journal of Occupational Therapy 26(3): 150–154.

Johnston, N. (1965). Group reading as a treatment tool with geriatrics. American Journal of Occupational Therapy 19(4): 192–195.

Kielhofner, G., and Burke, J. P. (1977). Occupational therapy after 60 years: An account of changing identity and knowledge. American Journal of Occupational Therapy 31(10): 674–689.

Kiernat, J. M. (1976). Geriatric day hospitals: A golden opportunity for therapists. American Journal of Occupational Therapy 30(5): 285–289.

Kiernat, J. M. (1979). The use of life review activity with confused nursing home residents. American Journal of Occupational Therapy 33(5): 306–310.

King, L. J. (1974). A sensory-integrative approach to schizophrenia. American Journal of Occupational Therapy 28(9): 529–536.

Koven, B., and Shuff, F. L. (1953). Group therapy with the chronically ill. American Journal of Occupational Therapy 7(5): 208–209, 219.

Kramer, L. W., and Beidel, D. C. (1982). Job seeking skills groups: A review and application to a chronic psychiatric population. Occupational Therapy in Mental Health: A Journal of Psychosocial Practice and Research 2(2): 37–44.

Kuenstler, G. (1976). A planning group for psychiatric outpatients. American Journal of Occupational Therapy 30(10): 634–639.

Labovitz, D. R. (1978). The returning therapist: A group approach. American Journal of Occupational Therapy 32(9): 580–585.

Lakin, M., and Dray, M. (1958). Psychological aspects of activity for the aged. American Journal of Occupational Therapy 12(4): 172–175, 187–188.

Lamb, R. H. (1967). Chronic psychiatric patients in the day hospital. Archives of General Psychiatry 17: 615–621.

Leuret, F. (1948). On the moral treatment of insanity. In S. Licht (ed. and trans.), Occupational Therapy Source Book. Baltimore: Williams & Wilkins. (Article originally written in 1840).

Levine, D., Marks, H. K., and Hall, R. (1957). Differential effect of factors in an activity therapy program. American Journal of Psychiatry 114: 532–535.

67

Licht, S. (ed.) (1948). Occupational Therapy Source Book. Baltimore: Williams & Wilkins.

Lindsay, W. P. (1983). The role of the occupational therapist in treatment of alcoholism. American Journal of Occupational Therapy 37(1): 36–43.

Linn, L., Weinroth, M. D., and Shamah, R. (1962). Occupational Therapy in Dynamic Psychiatry: An Introduction to the Four-Phase Concept in Hospital Psychiatry. Washington, DC: The American Psychiatric Association.

Linn, M. W., Caffey, E. M., Klett, C. J., Hogarty, G. E., and Lamb, H. R. (1979). Day treatment and psychotropic drugs in the aftercare of schizophrenic patients. Archives of General Psychiatry 36: 1055–1066.

Llorens, L. A. (1968). Changing methods in treatment of psychosocial dysfunction. American Journal of Occupational Therapy 22(1): 26–29.

Llorens, L. A., and Johnson, P. A. (1966). Occupational therapy in an ego-oriented milieu. American Journal of Occupational Therapy 20(4): 178–181.

Llorens, L. A., and Rubin, E. Z. (1967). Developing Ego Functions in Disturbed Children: Occupational Therapy in Milieu. Detroit: Wayne State University Press.

Lockerbie, L., and Stevenson, G. H. (1947). Socialization through occupational therapy. Occupational Therapy and Rehabilitation 26(3): 142–145.

Mahier, S. H., and Tachabrun, B. R. (1978). Experience and youth group: For elderly and adolescent psychiatric patients. American Journal of Occupational Therapy 32(2): 115–117.

Mann, W., Godfrey, M. E., and Dowd, E. T. (1973). The use of group counseling procedures in the rehabilitation of spinal cord injured patients. American Journal of Occupational Therapy 27(2): 73–77.

Markowitz, G. E., and Rosner, D. (1979). Doctors in crisis: Medical education and medical reform during the progressive era, 1895–1915. In S. Reverby and D. Rosner (eds.), Health Care in America: Essays in Social History. Philadelphia: Temple University Press.

Marsh, L. C. (1936). Group treatment of relatives of psychotic patients. Occupational Therapy and Rehabilitation 15(1): 1–17.

Maslen, D. (1982). Rehabilitation training for community living skills: Concepts and techniques. Occupational Therapy in Mental Health: A Journal of Psychosocial Practice and Research 2(1): 33–49.

Maynard, M., and Pedro, D. (1971). One day experience in group dynamics in an occupational therapy assistant course. American Journal of Occupational Therapy 25(3): 170–171.

Mazer, J. L. (Project Director) (1968). Final Report Rehabilitation Services Administration Grant #123–T–68 for Field Consultant in Psychiatric Rehabilitation. New York: American Occupational Therapy Association.

McKibbin, E., and King, J. (1983). Activity group counseling for learning-disabled children with behavior problems. American Journal of Occupational Therapy 37(9): 617–623.

Menks, F., Sittles, S., Weaver, D., and Yanow, B. (1977). A psychogeriatric activity group in a rural community. American Journal of Occupational Therapy 31(6): 376–384.

Meyer, A. (1977). The philosophy of occupational therapy. American Journal of Occupational Therapy 31(10): 639–642. (Originally published 1922).

Mosey, A. C. (1968). Recapitulation of ontogenesis: A theory for practice of occupational therapy. American Journal of Occupational Therapy 22(5): 426–432.

Mosey, A. C. (1969). Dependency and integrative skill as they relate to affinity for and acceptance by an assigned group. American Journal of Occupational Therapy 23(4): 348–349.

Mosey, A. C. (1970a). The concept and use of developmental groups. American Journal of Occupational Therapy 24(4): 272–275.

Mosey, A. C. (1970b). Three Frames of Reference for Mental Health. Thorofare, NJ: Charles B. Slack.

Mosey, A. C. (1971). Occupational therapy: A historical perspective. Involvement in the rehabilitation movement—1942–1960. American Journal of Occupational Therapy 25(5): 234–236.

Mosey, A. C. (1973a). Activities Therapy. New York: Raven Press.

Mosey, A. C. (1973b). Meeting health needs. American Journal of Occupational Therapy 27(1): 14–17.

Mosey, A. C. (1974). An alternative: The biopsychosocial model. American Journal of Occupational Therapy 28(3): 137–140.

Mosey, A. C. (1980). A model for occupational therapy. Occupational Therapy in Mental Health: A Journal of Psychosocial Practice and Research 1(1): 11–31.

Mosey, A. C. (1981). Occupational Therapy: Configuration of a Profession. New York: Raven Press.

Moss, F. B., and Stewart, G. (1959). A program for geriatric patients from hospital to community. American Journal of Occupational Therapy 13(6): 268–271.

Mumford, M. S. (1974). A comparison of interpersonal skills in verbal and activity groups. American Journal of Occupational Therapy 28(5): 281–283.

Neistadt, M. E., and Marques, K. (1984). An independent living skills training program. American Journal of Occupational Therapy 38(10): 671–676.

Nelson, A., Mackenthun, D., Bloesch, M., Milan, A., Unrein, M., and Hill, K. (1956). A preliminary report on a study in group occupational therapy. American Journal of Occupational Therapy 10(5): 254–258, 262–263, 271.

Neville, A. (1980). Temporal adaptation: Application with short-term psychiatric patients. American Journal of Occupational Therapy 34(5): 328–331.

Noce, S. F., Breuninger, P. L., and Noce, J. S. (1983). A Piagetian-based approach for the assessment and occupational therapy treatment of cognitive deficits in process schizophrenic and psychogeriatric patients. In W. E. Kelly (ed.), The Changing Role of Rehabilitation Medicine in the Management of the Psychiatric Patient. Springfield, IL: Charles C. Thomas.

Novick, L. J. (1961). Occupational therapy and social group work in the home for the sick aged: A comparison. American Journal of Occupational Therapy 15(5): 198–203, 211.

Odhner, F. (1970a). A study of group tasks as facilitators of verbalization among hospitalized schizophrenic patients. American Journal of Occupational Therapy 24(1): 7–12.

Odhner, F. (1970b). Group dynamics of the interdisciplinary team. American Journal of Occupational Therapy 24(7): 484–487.

Owen, C., and Newman, N. (1965). Utilizing films as a therapeutic agent in group interaction. American Journal of Occupational Therapy 19(4): 205–207.

Pasework, R. and Hornby, R. (1968). The effect upon social interaction patterns of a short-term stimulation program for psychiatric geriatric patients. American Journal of Occupational Therapy 22(3): 195–196.

Patterson, T. W., Marron, J. R., and Patterson, N. B. (1970). Behavioral patterns of occupational therapy students on the FIRO-B. American Journal of Occupational Therapy 24(4): 269–271.

Pearman, H. E., and Newman, N. (1968). Work-oriented occupational therapy for the geriatric patient. American Journal of Occupational Therapy 22(3): 203–208.

Posthuma, B. W. and Posthuma, A. B. (1972). The effect of a small-group experience on occupational therapy students. American Journal of Occupational Therapy 26(8): 415–418.

Rance, C., and Price, A. (1973). Poetry as a group project. American Journal of Occupational Therapy 27(5): 252–255.

Reed, K. L., and Sanderson, S. R. (1980). Concepts of Occupational Therapy. Baltimore: Williams & Wilkins.

70

Reilly, M. (1966). A psychiatric occupational therapy program as a teaching model. American Journal of Occupational Therapy 20(2): 61–67.

Rerek, M. D. (1971). Occupational therapy: A historical perspective The Depression years—1929 to 1941. American Journal of Occupational Therapy 25(5): 231–233.

Rider, B. B. and Gramlin, J. T. (1980). An activities approach to occupational therapy in a short-term acute mental health unit. American Occupational Therapy Association Mental Health Specialty Section Newsletter 3(4): Rockville, MD.

Rosner, D. (1979). Business at the bedside: Health care in Brooklyn, 1890–1915. In S. Reverby and D. Rosner (eds.), Health Care in America: Essays in Social History. Philadelphia: Temple University Press.

Ross, M., and Burdick, D. (1978). A Sensory Integration Training Manual for Regressed and Geriatric Patients. Middletown, CT: Department of Rehabilitation Services, Connecticut Valley Hospital.

Rothaus, P., Hanson, P. G., and Cleveland, S. E. (1966). Art and group dynamics. American Journal of Occupational Therapy 20(4): 182–187.

Rothman, D. J. (1980). Conscience and Convenience: The Asylum and its Alternatives in Progressive America. Boston: Little, Brown & Co.

Schiffer, M. (1979). The genealogy of group psychotherapy. In S. R. Slavson (author) and M. Schiffer (ed.), Dynamics of Group Psychotherapy. New York: Jason Aronson.

Schuman, S. H., Marcus, D., and Nesse, D. (1973). Puppetry and the mentally ill. American Journal of Occupational Therapy 27(8): 484–486.

Schwartzberg, S. L., Howe, M. C., and McDermott, A. (1982). Comparison of three treatment group formats for facilitating social interaction. Occupational Therapy in Mental Health: A Journal of Psychosocial Practice and Research 2(4): 1–16.

Shannon, P. D., and Snortum, J. R., (1965). An activity group's role in intensive psychotherapy. American Journal of Occupational Therapy 19(6): 344–347.

Slagle, E. C. (1922). Training aides for mental patients. Archives of Occupational Therapy 1(1): 11–17.

Slavson, S. R. (1979). Vita-Erg therapy with long-term, regressed psychotic women. In S. R. Slavson (author) and M. Schiffer (ed.), Dynamics of Group Psychotherapy. New York: Jason Aronson. (Article originally written in 1967).

Smuts, R. W. (1959). Women and Work in America. New York: Columbia University Press.

Solomon, A. P., and Fentress, T. L. (1947). A critical study of analytically oriented group psychotherapy utilizing the technique of dramatization of the psychodynamics. Occupational Therapy and Rehabilitation 26(1): 23–46.

Springfield, F. B., and Tullis, L. H. (1958). An intensive activities program for chronic neuropsychiatric patients. American Journal of Occupational Therapy 12(5): 247–249.

Stein, F. (1982). A current review of the behavioral frame of reference and its application to occupational therapy. Occupational Therapy in Mental Health: A Journal of Psychosocial Practice and Research 2(4): 35–62.

Steiner, J. (1972). Reflections on the encounter group and the therapist. American Journal of Occupational Therapy 26(3): 130–131.

Talbot, J. F. (1983). An inpatient adolescent living skills program. Occupational Therapy in Mental Health: A Journal of Psychosocial Practice and Research 3(4): 35–45.

VanderRoest, L. L., and Clements, S. T. (1983). Sensory Integration: Rationale and Treatment Activities for Groups. Grand Rapids, MI: South Kent Mental Health Services, Inc.

Versluys, H. (1980). The remediation of role disorders through focused group work. American Journal of Occupational Therapy 34(9): 609–614.

Webb, L. J. (1973). The therapeutic social club. American Journal of Occupational Therapy 27(2): 81–83.

Werner, V., Maddigan, R. F., and Watson, C. G. (1969). A study of two treatment programs for chronic mentally ill patients in occupational therapy. American Journal of Occupational Therapy 23(2): 132–136.

West, W. L. (ed.) (1959). Changing Concepts and Practices in Psychiatric Occupational Therapy. Dubuque, IA: William C. Brown.

White, C. V. (1953). Group projects with psychiatric patients. American Journal of Occupational Therapy 7(6): 253, 270.

Wiebe, R. H. (1967). The Search for Order 1877–1920. New York: Hill and Wang.

Wilson, L. G. (1979). The use of a stroke group treatment program on an extended care unit. The Canadian Journal of Occupational Therapy 46(1): 19–20.

Woodside, H. H. (1971). Occupational therapy—A historical perspective. The development of occupational therapy 1910–1929. American Journal of Occupational Therapy 25(5): 226–230.

3

Current Practice
in Occupational Therapy

A comprehensive view of occupational therapy groups requires both a broad historical picture and an assessment of contemporary practice. The brief history in Chapter 2 described the stages through which group work in occupational therapy has evolved. In the development of any discipline or institution one era builds upon an earlier one, so that the new exhibits characteristics of the earlier stage. So it is with the current era, the Era of Adaptation. While the emphasis in this era is on types of group treatment whose goals focus on problems of adaptation and on teaching skills necessary for adaptation, the group is still based on an understanding of group dynamics, an awareness of the importance of ego-building, and support for therapeutic and educational change.

  A variety of health care services is available to individuals residing in any given community. These services range from intensive inpatient care for acute illness in the long-term rehabilitation hospital; with various programs of partial hospitalization, out-patient services, and home or community-based programs. Patients may receive treatment in a number of different health care settings during the course of an illness. Therefore, individuals need to adapt as they move from one type of health care environment to another. Urie Bronfenbrenner (1979), a psychologist who studies the effects of environmental interaction on human development, refers to these changes of environment as ecological transitions. He adds that "an ecological transition occurs whenever a person's position in the ecological environment is altered as a result of a change in role, setting, or both" (p. 27). Growth and change do not take place in a vacuum; they are expressed through behavior that occurs in a particular environmental context. So it is that individuals must adapt in each context and environment of the health care service continuum.

Contemporary Types of Groups

Duncombe and Howe (1985), researchers in occupational therapy, sought to clarify the nature and scope of group work in their profession by surveying practicing occupational therapists. Questionnaires were mailed to 300 occupational therapists whose names were selected from the 1980 member yearbook of the American Occupational Therapy Association. Research results were based upon the responses of 120 currently employed therapists. The distribution of these respondents among work settings, geographical areas, and number of years of certification approximated the distribution of practicing therapists in the United States as a whole.

The questionnaire had three parts. The first part asked for information about the respondents; the second part dealt with whether or not the respondents used groups as a method of treatment, and if not, why not; and the third part was directed to those respondents who used groups in patient treatment. Respondents were requested to provide information on up to four treatment groups that they led and to complete a checklist on the characteristics and goals of the groups that they described. A group was defined as "an aggregate of people who share a common purpose which can be attained only by group members interacting and working together" (Mosey, 1973, p. 45).

In part one the respondents were asked to identify the types of health facilities where they worked (see Table 3-1). The largest number of therapists were employed by large general hospitals and schools, followed by rehabilitation centers and psychiatric hospitals. Of the 120 responding therapists, 72 used groups in treatment and 48 did not. Two reasons were cited for not using groups in treatment: (1) occupational therapy was provided only on a one-to-

TABLE 3-1.
INSTITUTIONS EMPLOYING OCCUPATIONAL THERAPISTS

Type of Facility	Total	Number in Which Therapists Use Groups	Number in Which Therapists Do Not Use Groups
1. Large general hospitals	25	13	12
2. Small general hospitals	8	7	1
3. Rehabilitation centers	16	7	9
4. Psychiatric hospitals	16	16	0
5. Community mental health centers	6	6	0
6. Nursing homes	5	2	3
7. Community programs	8	4	4
8. Schools	22	10	12
9. Mental retardation facilities	8	4	4
10. Miscellaneous	6	3	3
TOTALS	120	72	48

Adapted from Duncombe, L., and Howe, M. C. (1985). Group work in occupational therapy: A survey of practice. *American Journal of Occupational Therapy* 39(3): p. 165.

one basis in the therapist's facility (42%) or (2) the patient population was not deemed suitable for group treatment (36%). All the respondents working in psychiatric hospitals and community mental health centers reported using groups in treatment. The use of groups was reported in all other types of treatment facilities, in varying degrees, as shown in Figure 3-1.

Of greatest interest is the information gathered on the 209 groups led by the respondents in the study. The researchers state, "Fifty-four percent (109) of the groups were labeled activity groups and 24% (48) were labeled verbal groups. A chi-square analysis showed that there was a significantly greater number of activity groups than verbal groups (12.1, df1, P ≤ .01). Also, 76% of the groups were reported to be small groups of ten members or less. The most common size was six to ten members. A chi-square analysis confirmed that there were significantly more groups with ten or less members than groups of more than ten members (31.9, df1, P ≤ .01)" (pp. 165–166).

On the basis of the descriptions of the groups, the researchers established ten categories of groups. The researchers were guided in identifying group types by the respondents' names for the groups and their designated activities. Although the groups fell into ten categories, there were clearly some areas of overlap in the activities used. Overlapping is characteristic of the flexibility required in practice. The ten types of groups were the exercise group; four types of task groups, namely, cooking group, task group, activities of daily living group, and arts and crafts group; the self-expression group; two types of discussion groups, namely, the feeling-oriented discussion group and the reality-oriented discussion group; the sensori-motor or sensory integration group; and the educational group. Duncombe and Howe developed brief descriptions of these groups from respondents' replies on the questionnaire.

Exercise Group

Members of exercise groups were involved in doing physical exercises to increase their coordination, mobility, and strength. Group activities were games involving ball play such as catch, volleyball, ping pong, and bowling. Also included were recreational sports, "new games," and dance or movement activities. Members often participated in these activities from a chair or a wheelchair. Group size varied from six to as many as 20 participants. They were usually adults (65%)

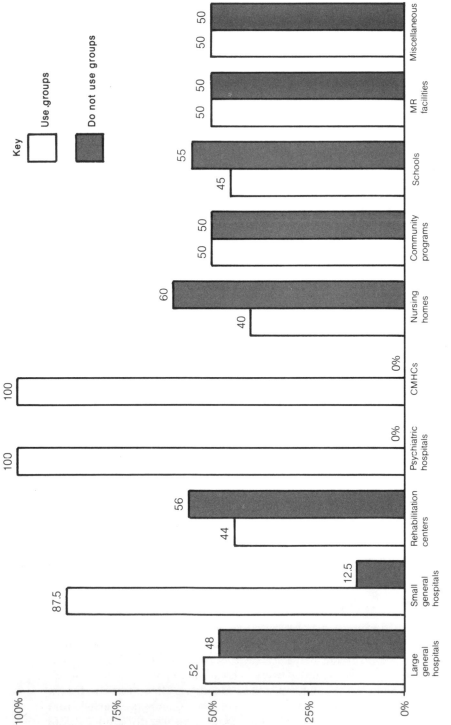

FIG. 3-1. Percentage comparison of the use of groups by facility. (Adapted from Duncombe, L., and Howe, M. C. (1985). Group work in occupational therapy: A survey of practice. American Journal of Occupational Therapy, 39(3):165.)

with psychosocial, physical, or developmental disabilities. Exercise groups were most frequently found in rehabilitation centers and schools for the developmentally delayed. Goals for the exercise groups were primarily therapeutic—to increase physical abilities (100%) and to facilitate communication and socialization (88%).

Cooking Group

Cooking groups usually combined the tasks of planning, shopping, cooking, and eating the meal. These groups, with five to eight members, often cooked a meal for a much larger group. A majority of the cooking groups were in therapy programs for adult and adolescent psychiatric patients, commonly with a diagnosis of schizophrenia. Cooking groups were also found in rehabilitation programs with adult spinal cord injuries, arthritis, and neurological conditions. These were short-term, open or closed groups with specific goals of facilitating communication and socialization (94%), increasing task skills (85%), educating and sharing information. Cooking groups were ordinarily found in psychiatric programs and in large general hospitals.

Activities of Daily Living Group

The activities of daily living category contained the largest number (17%) of groups. Two thirds of the living skills groups were conducted in hospitals for adults with psychosocial dysfunctions. The remaining number, in rehabilitation centers, were conducted for adults with spinal cord injuries, head and neurological injuries, stroke, and cardiovascular disease. In both settings the groups shared two different sets of goals. Some groups worked on predischarge living skills and on preparing for independent living in the community. Other groups concentrated on developing living skills for greater independence in self-care within the institution. The daily living skills groups were predominantly closed, short-term activity groups with three to eight members. The specific goals in the groups were to increase task skills (80%), and to share information (78%).

Arts and Crafts Group

Arts and crafts groups were used for the evaluation and treatment of psychosocial disorders. Patients usually worked on individual projects within the group setting. Some of the groups, particularly those concerned with the evaluation of existing skills, were small, with less than five members. Other groups, concerned with developing leisure skills, were as large as 15 members. These groups were closed, adult activity groups designed to increase task skills (90.5%) and to promote socialization and communication between members (76%).

Task Group

Task groups included groups that met to create a product other than a meal. They were used most often with adult psychiatric patients and with patients with developmental disabilities. Two types of tasks were undertaken: group tasks, such as publishing a newsletter or a yearbook, or planning and holding a recreational or social event; and a prevocational or work-related assembly and production project within the treatment facility, such as the one in Figure 3-2. Some of the task groups were small, with only six to ten members, but the prevocational, production work-related groups were larger, with as many as 20 members. The task groups were long-term, closed activity groups for adults; goals were to increase socialization and communication (82%) and to increase task skills (77%).

Self-expression Group

The self-expression group was reported primarily by the occupational therapists working with adult patients who had psychosocial problems. The media of the self-expression groups were music, art, role playing, and self-awareness exercises. The groups were both open and closed, short-term verbal groups with less than ten members. The specific goals were socialization and communication (91%) and to achieve insight (81%).

Feeling-Oriented Discussion Group

The feeling-oriented discussion groups were found in psychiatric programs with schizophrenic and manic-depressive adults who were not psychotic. Some groups were designated as group psychotherapy. Role playing, poetry, and fantasy were used to promote discussion. These were verbal groups of six to ten adults, and the group goals were to provide support, to increase communication and socialization, and to achieve insight.

FIG. 3-2. A work related group load their product for delivery. (Courtesy of the Towne House Creative Living Center, Oakland, CA)

Reality-Oriented Discussion Group

The reality-oriented discussion group was designed for adults with psychosocial dysfunction. The topics for discussion included current events in the daily news, events occurring within the program, individual treatment goals, use of time, and program and discharge planning. Some groups used specific group techniques such as transactional analysis, assertiveness training, and role playing. Groups varied in size from four to ten members. They were predominantly verbal, short-term, open or closed adult groups. The goals were to increase communication and socialization (93%) and to provide education and share information (71%).

Sensori-motor and Sensory Integration Group

Sensori-motor and sensory integration groups were usually for children who were receiving group treatment in school programs—preschool through high school. The problems ranged from learning disabilities, cerebral palsy, and developmental disabilities to sensory integrative disorders and auditory and visual problems. Group members participated in gross motor and fine motor activities as well as tactile, taste, and vestibular stimulation. The groups were small in size, under five members. They were predominantly long-term activity groups for elementary school-aged children. Primary goals were to develop physical abilities (85%) and sensory integration (85%). Secondary goals were to provide opportunities for communication and socialization (75%).

82

Educational Group

The majority of the educational groups were for parents and families of individuals who were receiving treatment. Also included were groups that provided information and discussion on medications, joint protection for arthritis, and family planning. These were verbal, short-term groups for adults ranging in size from as few as four members to as many as 20 members. Specific goals were to provide support and meet health needs (100%) and to provide education and share information (77%).

Contemporary Issues

The evidence gathered about group work in contemporary occupational therapy practice by Duncombe and Howe underscores a number of important issues. The majority of occupational therapy groups were planned around an activity. Even when the group meetings were primarily for discussion, the members were talking about activity or occupation. Clearly the profession is still firmly rooted in the development of the Project Era.

The definition of occupational therapy has come to include specific objectives. Therapists must seek to restore, reinforce, and enhance the performance of skills and functions essential for adaptation. It was not surprising, therefore, that Duncombe and Howe found that groups for activities of daily living were the most frequently reported by the therapists surveyed. When cooking groups are added to the activities of daily living groups, the two types of groups comprise one fourth of the total number of all groups. Furthermore, for all categories except the self-expression and the feeling-oriented discussion groups, therapists ranked as one of their top two goals increasing skills, including those related to specific tasks, cognition, and physical abilities.

Therapists also ranked as one of their top two priorities facilitating communication and socialization among group members and in the environment beyond the group. Clearly, communication is an essential component of group participation, and increased communication contributes to greater learning from the group experience. Socialization also involves an interactive process between individuals. Through the socialization process, rules and models for social conduct, as well as behaviors needed for adaptation to changing environments, are transmitted. In her presentation of concepts from socialization theory, Burke (1983) states, "Socialization offers the useful perspective that persons acquire behavior in a process of being exposed to role models, expectations, demands for performance and information about performance. Socialization aids development of new and appropriate thinking and behaving throughout the life span. . . ." (p. 136). In the Era of Adaptation, socialization plays an important part in helping the individual adjust to a new environment. Thus, communication and socialization have an essential role in assisting the individual in both the learning and the adaptation processes.

Among these occupational therapy groups, educational goals as well as therapeutic group goals ranked high. Therapists commonly designed groups with multiple goals—nearly half of the therapists indicated that they sought to make their groups both educational and therapeutic. They sought to meet the goals that individual group members held for the group as well as the goals that the group had established for itself through a process shared by all members. All of the groups in the Duncombe and Howe study were reported to have multiple goals, that is, group as well as individual treatment goals.

In Chapter 2 we reported that membership in occupational therapy groups was often related to one of three factors: diagnosis, roles, or setting. Although the categories defined by Duncombe and

Howe did not closely agree with the three types thought to be typical of the Adaptation Era (in Chapter 2), therapists reported that about twice as many of their groups contained members with various diagnoses than groups with members restricted to one particular diagnostic group. An analysis of the group descriptions reported by the occupational therapists also revealed a strong trend toward role-focused groups. Over half of the groups were reported to have specific role-directed goals. Group goals were to support and enhance members' skills and functioning in such roles as workers, student, homemaker, family member, spouse, parent, adult, adolescent, and elder. Men's and women's groups addressed support for sex roles. A more general role orientation was evident in groups designed to increase independent living skills and leisure skills. Finally, occupational therapists did not always clearly identify the setting in which the group goals were to be realized. Settings identified as pertinent to the group goals include the postdischarge setting, the current hospital setting of patients, and the community setting. In response to the current trend toward short-term hospitalization and frequent changes in the treatment setting, occupational therapy groups now focus more on the roles and skills needed by the individual to adapt successfully to the new treatment environments.

Conclusion

The current variety of group work in occupational therapy points to the continuing evolution of group work as a therapeutic tool as well as indicating the flexibility available to therapists in designing group formats. By adhering to principles discovered in earlier years and applying modern research, therapists have devised a number of group formats to deal with specific problems. As therapists and researchers continue to explore the potential of group treatment, we can expect other formats to be designed and developed.

References

Bronfenbrenner, U. (1979). The Ecology of Human Development: Experiments by Nature and Design. Cambridge, MA: Harvard University Press.

Burke, J. P. (1983). Defining occupation: Importing and organizing inter-
    disciplinary knowledge. In G. Kielhofner (ed.), Health Through
    Occupation: Theory and Practice in Occupational Therapy. Phil-
    adelphia: F. A. Davis.
Duncombe, L., and Howe, M. C. (1985). Group work in occupational therapy:
    A survey of practice. American Journal of Occupational Therapy
    39(3): 163–170
Mosey, A. C. (1973). Activities Therapy. New York: Raven Press.

4

A Model
for Group Work

In the preceding chapters we described many different kinds of groups and examined their characteristics and overall goals. This chapter describes a model for an occupational therapy group; the model is entitled the functional group. The functional group, based on a functional approach to group work, is empirically derived from clinical experience and research, and is being introduced here in detail for the first time.

The functional group model is presented in accordance with a framework established by Reed (1984). In her description of the process of developing practice models, Reed identifies eight elements fundamental to the process: (1) the frame of reference, (2) assumptions, (3) concepts, (4) expected results of intervention, (5) assessment instruments, (6) intervention strategies, (7) logical deductions, and (8) intervention principles. At present, the functional group model is incomplete in a strict sense. For although it is based on empirical data, the model has not been formally tested, and we therefore lack the final element: intervention principles. Nevertheless, the model still functions to organize occupational therapy group practice, education, and research.

Framework of the Model

Frame of Reference

The functional group model is based on research in five areas related to occupational therapy: (1) group dynamics, (2) effectance, (3) needs hierarchy, (4) purposeful activity, and (5) adaptation. Group dynamics, the domain of social scientists, concerns the interrelationships of persons in a small group. The belief that a psychological field, like an energy field, acts upon and affects the behavior of a group was raised by Kurt Lewin in the 1930s (Knowles and Knowles, 1972). "Effectance" refers to the belief that individuals are drawn toward activity and that this behavior is self-motivated. The term "needs hierarchy" refers to the belief that humans have many needs and these are arranged in order of importance. Purposeful activity has come to be recognized as closely related to satisfaction of needs, and adaptation is recognized as one goal of this activity. Let us examine more closely each of these five areas.

Much of the early literature on group dynamics was important to developing the functional group model. By understanding the normal group, we formulated ideas about the therapy group and then the functional group (see Table 4-1). Concepts central to the beliefs regarding group dynamics were derived from Bales' work on interaction analysis (1950) and Benne and Sheats' description of group membership and leadership functions (1978). More recent works on group dynamics, such as those on group cohesiveness (Cartwright and Zander, 1968; Yalom, 1970), the phases of group development (Bennis and Shepard, 1956; Garland, Jones, and Kolodny, 1965; Tuckman, 1965), and individual growth through group process (Lifton, 1961) were also used to develop the model.

If we understand how persons within groups interact, we can increase the benefits of group participation for individuals. We should keep in mind several basic principles of group dynamics:

1. Groups have a common goal and dynamic interaction between members.
2. Groups provide multiple feedback and support.
3. Groups promote independence from and decreased dependence on an externally designated leader in a developmental progression.
4. Groups support growth and change of members.
5. Groups have a capacity for self-direction.
6. Groups can satisfy individual needs and social demands.

Robert White's work on "effectance motivation," or the "urge towards competence" (1959, 1971), was also central to the development of our model. Simply stated, White believed that exploratory behavior was self-motivated; he coined the term *effectance* to describe this motivation. This behavior had "adaptive value," White said (1959). "Effectance motivation must be conceived to involve satisfaction — a feeling of efficacy — in transactions in which behavior has an exploratory, varying, experimental character. . . . the behavior leads the organism to find out how the environment can be changed and what consequences flow from these changes" (p. 329). Maslow (1970) also attempted to explain motivation. According to him, humans have "intrinsic growth tendencies."

Maslow stated that people have "basic needs" that are organized in a hierarchy. These basic needs are: (1) physiological needs, (2) safety needs, (3) belongingness and love needs, (4) esteem needs, and (5) self-actualization needs. In Maslow's view, unsatisfied needs are a source of motivation; the individual puts his or her

TABLE 4-1.
FUNCTIONAL GROUP CORRELATES

Normal Group (nonspecific)	Therapy Group (more specific)	Functional Group (occupation specific)
Groups have a common goal and dynamic interaction between members.	Through use of the information base available in a group, members are provided with a here-and-now, reality orientation that encourages growth and change.	Groups can enhance the use of occupations to help people function independently, that is, adapt to the environment or adapt the environment to them.
Groups provide multiple feedback and support.	Groups are designed to give the amount and type of feedback and support that members need.	Feedback and support are part of the process of doing and participating, in the group activities selected to meet individual and social needs.
Groups promote independence and decreased dependence on an externally designated leader in a developmental progression.	Group discussions and activities can be structured to encourage group-centered leadership.	Structuring activities and the environment so that nonhuman objects lead the action gives members an opportunity to learn about what the environment can do and their own capabilities.
Through participation in group activities, groups can support growth and change of members.	Through discussion and participation in growth activities, groups can encourage and promote growth and change of members.	By selecting activities that permit practice and learning of skills needed to achieve mastery and competency, groups can provide opportunities for growth and change of members.
Groups have a capacity for self-direction.	Groups can be organized to accommodate many levels of human development and functioning.	Enabling the group to lead the doing, by giving members a set of possibilities, empowers the group's capacity for self-direction.
Groups can satisfy individual needs and social demands.	Through discussion and activities, groups can satisfy individual needs and provide learning necessary for the fulfillment of social demands.	Groups can be used to maintain, improve, or enhance the occupational nature of people by providing members an opportunity to deal with the real functions of objects.

energies into satisfying needs, dealing with the various needs in the order given.

Mosey (1973) similarly described a needs hierarchy in her concept of "health needs." She noted, "health needs are defined as inherent human requirements that must be met in order for an individual to experience a sense of physical, psychological, and social well-being" (p. 14). In Mosey's terminology, these needs are psychophysical, security, love and acceptance, group association, esteem, sexual, developmental, and pleasure (pp. 14–15). Mosey believes that a "need-satisfying environment" is an essential backdrop to a treatment program oriented toward change. Because patients are often unable to meet their own health needs, the occupational therapist must engineer need-satisfying environments in conjunction with change-oriented programs.

An idea central to the functional group model is purposeful activity. King (1978) defines purposeful activities as those that encourage an "adaptive response." In Reed's (1984) view, purposeful activities, or "meaningful occupations," give direction to "goal-oriented" behavior. Although Reed acknowledges that the definition of a term like *meaningful* is usually subjective, she states that "among the possible needs or demands which activities could fulfill are physiologic, security, belonging, societal and self actualizing needs" (p. 502). Regardless of the needs they fulfill, according to Reed, purposeful activities have an intent and are practical in daily living.

Csikszentmihalyi (1975), in his study of intrinsic rewards and motivation, gives further insight into the purpose or value of activity. He believes that people experience a "flow state" when their "skills match with the opportunities for action in the environment" (p. 177). When there is a mismatch, stress, anxiety, worry, or boredom may result. Fidler and Fidler (1978) explain purposeful action in their concept of "doing." "*Doing* is viewed as enabling the development and integration of the sensory, motor, cognitive, and psychological systems; serving as a socializing agent, and verifying one's efficacy as a competent, contributing member of one's society" (p. 305). They also emphasize that "both the quality and variety of *doing* is critical for ego development and adaptation" (p. 308). Barris, Kielhofner, and Hawkins (1983) also point out that intrinsically motivated behaviors lead to feelings of personal satisfaction.

Finally, to varying degrees all of the literature cited above touches on human adaptation. According to Burke (1983), "*occupation* [is] . . . *a behavior which is motivated by an intrinsic, conscious urge to be effective in the environment in order to enact a variety of individually interpreted roles that are shaped by cultural tradition and learned through the process of socialization*" (p. 136). For Reed (1984) "adaptation through occupation . . . means the organization and management of occupational activities and tasks in a manner that meets the goal of achieving maximum autonomy or functional independence, actualization or satisfaction and accomplishment" (p. 495). King (1978) and Fidler and Fidler (1978) see purposeful activity, or "doing," as primary to adaptation. White (1959) surmises that "effectance motivation" has adaptive value, and Maslow (1970) considers "basic needs" as intrinsic to the organization of adaptive human behavior—physiological, psychological, and social.

As stated above, the frame of reference for the functional group model includes research findings on group dynamics, effectance, needs hierarchy, purposeful activity, and adaptation. In addition, there is a significant relationship between these beliefs (K. L. Reed, personal communication, July 22, 1984). The model assumes a relationship between groups, therapy, and occupation. By examining the normal (nonspecific) group, we can better grasp variations in the therapy (more specific) group and then apply the concepts to the functional (occupation specific) group (see Table 4-1).

Assumptions

Assumptions are ideas we accept as valid or true without proof or logical support. Each of us accepts certain assumptions whether or not we are aware of doing so. Again following Reed's (1984) framework for model development, we describe here the assumptions in forming the functional group model. The assumptions are organized into four groups: man, health, occupation, and therapy.

In this model we make nine assumptions about people.

1. People are bio-psycho-social systems.
2. People are social beings and therefore exist in groups.
3. People are action- or "doing-" oriented, motivated toward competency.
4. People have needs that can be met through the give and take of a social system such as a group.
5. People communicate socially (interact) both verbally and nonverbally.
6. Growth and change are processes inherent in life.

7. People are unique, complete individuals, with wholeness or congruence between emotion and action.
8. Groups exist as models of the social behavior patterns in the larger society.
9. Groups mobilize powerful forces that have important effects on people as individuals: senses of identity are shaped by groups; positions in the group affect safety and self-esteem; and group membership may be highly valued or seen as a burden to the individual.

In this model we make four assumptions about health. First, an individual's state of health involves mind, body (internal), and physical environment—the individual in interaction with the social and physical environment. Second, purposeful activity supports the health of mind and body in an individual and in a collective being. Third, health involves a state of independence and capacity for self-direction. Fourth, health involves a state of interdependence and capacity for relatedness.

In this model we make six assumptions about occupation.

1. Directed purposeful occupations used in a group experience encourage the person to assume responsibility for meeting individual needs.
2. Purposeful activities involve choice or volition by the individual and group toward a goal or purpose.
3. Purposeful activities, or occupations, used in a group experience are useful in improving the performance level and adaptive behavior of the person, and thus increasing potential for meeting individual responsibilities.
4. Active doing (involvement) in a group encourages the maintenance, development, and redevelopment of skills in areas of self-care, productivity (work), and leisure (play).
5. Through active doing in a group experience the individual gains a sense of self-worth and self-appraisal.
6. Lack of purposeful activity or idleness in a group leads to disorientation and break-down in habits, and thus threatens the individual health of both mind and body.

Finally, in this model, we make three assumptions about therapy. First, occupational therapy conducted in a group involves the use of directed, purposeful occupations, or activities, to positively influence a person's sense of well-being or state of health. Second, occupational therapy conducted in a group elicits an adaptive response and thereby requires a positive role that involves active participation, requires the person to meet the environmental demands of needs, tasks, and goals, permits subcortical centers to integrate and organize a response, and leads to self-reinforcement (King, 1978). Third, occupational therapy conducted in a group attempts to satisfy individual biological, psychological, and social requirements in conjunction with efforts to influence change in the person's state of health.

Concepts

At the heart of the model is a set of concepts that define the model in precise terms. The basic concepts here are adaptation and occupation (or action) and its four different forms: purposeful action, self-initiated action, spontaneous or here-and-now action, and group-centered action.

The functional group is defined by the use of time and energy in action designed to promote adaptation. The term *adaptation* is defined as the adjustment of the organism to its environment, or the process by which it adjusts (Reed and Sanderson, 1983). *Fitness* and *health* are terms used to describe a state of adaptation. The characteristics of adaptation (King, 1978) have been translated into the functional group model shown in Table 4-2.

Adaptation is brought about through occupation or action. Thus, the functional group model is action-oriented: members of the group are either directly involved in action or engaged in discussion about action. This orientation stems from the belief that behavior is a manifestation of the person as a whole, and in health a congruence between emotion and action is sought. This belief is based on the view that human beings are action-oriented, and that "doing" is basic to their nature.

There are four types of action in the functional group model. First, action must be *purposeful:* the activity must be recognized by the individuals and the group as congruent with their needs and goals. Fidler and Fidler (1983) explain that "mastery and competence are verified and become obvious in the reality of an end product. When the product resulting from an activity has social and cultural relevance to the individual and to his or her social groups, meaning is enhanced and social efficacy is affirmed" (p. 277). In

TABLE 4-2.
ADAPTATION AND THE FUNCTIONAL GROUP MODEL

Characteristics of Adaptation*	Functional Group Model
Requires a role that involves active participation	Group empowers maximum involvement through interaction between members, a common goal, and a task. Group mobilizes powerful forces that have important effects on member's sense of individual and group indentity.
Requires person to meet the environmental demands of needs, tasks, and goals	Group promotes independence and capacity for self-direction through the support and safety of group members. Group promotes action flow and experience. Group contains occupational component as well as social component.
Permits subcortical centers to integrate and organize a response	Group focuses on the here-and-now group task thus learning organization of input and output to subcortical centers of individuals. Group spontaneously involves members in the action.
Leads to self-reinforcement	Group membership support and feedback provides consensual validation for learning. Group builds on strengths.

*King, L. J. (1978). 1978 Eleanor Clarke Slagle Lecture: Toward a science of adaptive responses. American Journal of Occupational Therapy 32(7): 429–437. Reprinted with the permission of the American Occupational Therapy Association, Inc.

addition, the activity must be suitable to the group members and their available skills. Finally, the human and nonhuman objects and environment related to the activity must be considered. Certain environments and objects may represent attitudes or feelings about one's degree of control, compliance, inclusion, or desirability. Fidler and Fidler (1983) explain, "when there is congruency between individual characteristics and the real and symbolic characteristics of an activity, there is greater likelihood that the doing experience will result in a feeling of pleasure and personal satisfaction, and that the essential learning will be integrated as an adaptive response" (p. 277).

Second, action must be *self-initiated*, that is, individuals must seek to improve their skills or understanding and seek a group on their own volition. If individuals do not personally choose to join or participate in the group, they will not achieve the goals they seek.

Third, *spontaneous or here-and-now* action is essential; functional groups are based on experience, on experiential learning in the present. These groups provide a supportive environment, a place in which to practice living skills. Rather than focusing on the past, the group provides a place for members to function in the present and to practice skills in decision making, judgment, and perception as well as in areas of special deficits. Through spontaneous action, emphasis is placed on learning in the present.

Fourth, action must be *group-centered*, a major distinguishing feature of the functional group. The group structure and goals *always* take into consideration the emotional and social needs of all members. The group leader aims to create an environment that encourages interdependent action through consensus. Group-centered action allows maximal involvement through the interaction of all members, including leaders, working toward a common goal and task. Through group-centered action, powerful forces that have important effects on members' sense of individual and group identity are mobilized. These forces permit, enable, or enhance self-initiated, purposeful, and spontaneous action.

The implications of the concepts forming the core of the functional group model are summarized below. See Figure 4-1 for a schematic representation of the model.

We may make five statements about functional groups as social systems.

1. Functional groups provide a structure to guide the individual's participation. The structure and goals always address the social and emotional needs of the individual and are therefore said to be ego-oriented.
2. Groups intrinsically provide special therapeutic benefit, since occupational behavior is learned and shaped through a process of socialization.
3. Functional group activities build on strengths of the individual in the group; therefore, there is interest in the strengths and weaknesses of each member.

Composition
LEVEL OF FUNCTION
PROBLEM/DIAGNOSIS
ROLE
AGE, SEX, SOCIO-ECONOMIC STATUS
FINANCIAL RESOURCES
LEADER

Meta-Characteristics
group climate-setting
phases (group course)
structure of group:
    size
    open vs. closed
    duration, etc.

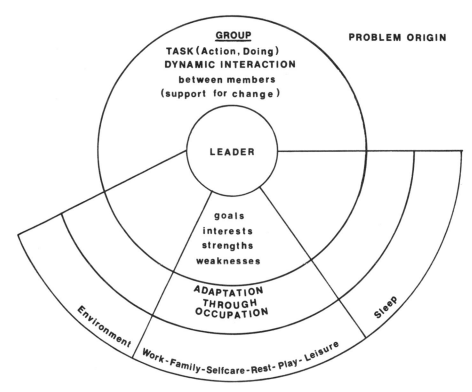

FIG. 4-1. Representation of the functional group model.

4. Functional groups can parallel and reflect the needs of the individual and the demands of society.

5. Functional groups are assumed to provide benefits to members through mutual help. Groups are therefore structured so that members have the opportunity to help each other,

thus enhancing members' perceptions and feelings of self-worth.

We may make three statements about functional groups as agents of change.

1. Groups can motivate people to action; functional groups are structured to motivate members to purposeful and meaningful action.
2. Functional groups are experience-based groups, in which experiential learning occurs in the here-and-now. These groups provide a supportive environment, a place in which to practice living skills.
3. Functional groups attempt to move members from dependence to independence or function and from maladaptation to adaptation.

We may make three statements about the functional orientation of the functional group.

1. Functional groups provide a place for members to function in the reality of the present and to practice skills in decision making, judgment, and perception, as well as in areas of special deficits.
2. Functional groups are concerned with elements of performance as well as with types of performance, such as work, play, and self-maintenance.
3. Functional groups seek to build group cohesiveness; a certain degree of cohesiveness is necessary to achieve functional goals.

We may make four statements about the action component of the functional group.

1. The goal of the functional group is not the product of the group, even though the group may have a meaningful product, but rather that learning process which occurs through active participation.
2. Functional groups nurture interpersonal and intrapersonal development through activity choice, climate, and goals.

3. Functional groups make use of both the human and non-human environment and object relations. Attention is directed to attachments to people and objects as well as to separations from people and objects.
4. Functional group leaders are cognizant of the individual's need for self-motivation and desire for mastery. They guide the activity of the group accordingly.

Expected Results of Intervention

The goal of the functional group is to promote health or adaptation through purposeful, self-initiated, spontaneous, group-centered action. A group can have multiple goals, thus incorporating the specific needs and goals of individual members as well as those more general goals and needs shared by all members.

The population served by the functional group are persons with physical illness or injury, emotional disorders, congenital or developmental disabilities, or problems precipitated by the aging process. The group can achieve specific goals in two categories: evaluation and the treatment process. First, the functional group provides an opportunity for observation and evaluation of behavior and interaction with the human and nonhuman environment for purposes of diagnosing performance problems. Second, the functional group is structured to motivate members to act in order to achieve optimal function and adaptation, prevent occupational deficits, and maintain and promote health and well-being.

The functional group can be described as providing group experience in which (1) objects lead action, (2) action is used to enhance individual member's well-being and sense of internal control, (3) talking is used to clarify doing, and (4) the therapist is teaching members to lead.

The functional group may also be characterized by what it is not. First, it is not *a leaderless group*. The group leader plays an important role in facilitating the group process and in planning for the group sessions. Second, it is not *group psychotherapy*. While the functional group model is designed to provide therapy for patients with problems in the psychosocial area, it does not focus on, nor is it primarily concerned with, developing insight through surfacing repressed or unconscious material. Third, it is not an *activity therapy group*. According to Slavson (1950), the founder of activity therapy, the goal of the activity therapy group is to bring about relief of "characterological" pathology (p. 2). The functional group seeks to enhance occupational behavior and thus adaptation. Fourth, it is not *focused on etiology*. The functional group does not focus on, or seek to alter, the etiology of a condition but rather facilitates change in the symptoms of a given condition as they interfere with occupation and adaptation. The emphasis is not on the diagnostic categories and symptoms because they are manifested in different ways in different individuals and the expectation of a particular symptomatology may well impede the therapeutic progress for the group and the individual.

Assessment Instruments

Methods of assessment are developed to collect data and information for determining whether certain problems exist and what intervention strategy to use (Reed, 1984). The assessment instruments used in the functional group are discussed in Chapters 5 through 9. They include observation (verbal and nonverbal), content and process analysis, needs assessment, group protocol, observation guides for initial evaluation, and observation guides for assessing ongoing group function and structure (*e.g.*, sociogram, member behavior rating forms, and group evaluation forms). In addition, group members are encouraged to be observers and evaluators in order to determine the validity of leader assessments.

Intervention Strategies

Intervention strategies are the media, modalities, methods, techniques, and equipment used to bring about change in the patient and achieve specific goals or objectives (Reed, 1984). Again, these strategies are detailed in Chapters 5 through 9, and include defining issues and expectations during the course of the group and using purposeful, self-initiated, spontaneous, group-centered action.

Logical Deductions

If the model is effective in bringing about change and achieving the stated goals, we can deduce certain results. The logical deductions are stated as hypotheses in question or answer form (Reed, 1984). If one implements the functional group model, we can expect the following results:

1. Group members' health needs will be met.
2. Group members will learn the skills and occupational behaviors necessary for adaptation.

Intervention Principles

According to Reed (1984), generalizations about the accuracy of a model must be derived from the results of tests of the hypotheses. These generalizations are the intervention principles. Although the functional group model is based on empirical evidence, this stage is not yet complete. At present we can only say that there is some evidence in the occupational therapy literature to support our hypotheses (Henry, Nelson, and Duncombe, 1984; Mumford, 1974; Odhner, 1970; Schwartzberg, Howe, and McDermott, 1982). The relevant research will be discussed in Chapter 10.

Conclusion

The functional group model is an occupational therapy approach to group work, and represents a new model of practice. It is based in part on the work of practitioners and researchers in preceding decades and in part on the recognition of current needs in the field of occupational therapy. The framework presented serves as a guide; answers posed to new or difficult questions can be measured against the statements in the relevant categories.

References

Bales, R. F. (1950). Interaction Process Analysis: A Method for the Study of Small Groups. Cambridge: Addison-Wesley.

Barris, R., Kielhofner, G., and Hawkins, J. H. (1983). Psychosocial Occupational Therapy: Practice in a Pluralistic Arena. Laurel, MD: Ramsco.

Benne, K. D., and Sheats, P. (1978). Functional roles of group members. In L. P. Bradford (ed.), Group Development (2nd ed.), pp. 52–61. La Jolla, CA; University Associates.

Bennis, W. B., and Shepard, H. A. (1956). A theory of group development. Human Relations 9(4): 415–457.

Burke, J. P. (1983). Defining occupation: Importing and organizing interdisciplinary knowledge. In G. Kielhofner (ed.), Health Through

Occupation: Theory and Practice in Occupational Therapy, pp. 125–138. Philadelphia: F. A. Davis.

Cartwright, D., and Zander, A. (eds.) (1968). Group Dynamics Research and Theory (3rd ed.). New York: Harper & Row.

Csikszentmihalyi, M. (1975). Beyond Boredom and Anxiety: The Experience of Play in Work and Games. San Francisco: Jossey-Bass.

Fidler, G. S., and Fidler, J. W. (1978). Doing and becoming: Purposeful action and self-actualization. American Journal of Occupational Therapy 32(5): 305–310.

Fidler, G. S., and Fidler, J. W. (1983). Doing and becoming: The occupational therapy experience. In G. Kielhofner (ed.), Health through Occupation: Theory and Practice in Occupational Therapy, pp. 267–280. Philadelphia: F. A. Davis.

Garland, J. A., Jones, H. E., and Kolodny, R. (1965). A Model for Stages of Development in Social Work. Boston: Boston University School of Social Work.

Henry, A. D., Nelson, D. L., and Duncombe, L. W. (1984). Choice making in group and individual activity. American Journal of Occupational Therapy 38(4): 245–251.

King, L. J. (1978). 1978 Eleanor Clarke Slagle Lecture: Toward a science of adaptive responses. American Journal of Occupational Therapy 32(7): 429–437.

Knowles, M., and Knowles, H. (1972). Introduction to Group Dynamics (rev. ed.). New York: Association Press.

Lifton, W. M. (1961). Working with groups: Group Process and Individual Growth. New York: John Wiley & Sons.

Maslow, A. H. (1970). Motivation and Personality (2nd ed.). New York: Harper & Row.

Mosey, A. C. (1973). Meeting health needs. American Journal of Occupational Therapy 27(1): 14–17.

Mumford, M. S. (1974). A comparison of interpersonal skills in verbal and activity groups. American Journal of Occupational Therapy 28(5): 281–283.

Odhner, F. (1970). A study of group tasks as facilitators of verbalization among hospitalized schizophrenic patients. American Journal of Occupational Therapy 24(1): 7–12.

Reed, K. L. (1984). Models of Practice in Occupational Therapy. Baltimore: Williams & Wilkins.

Reed, K. L., and Sanderson, S. (1983). Concepts of Occupational Therapy (2nd ed.). Baltimore: Williams & Wilkins.

Schwartzberg, S. L., Howe, M. C., and McDermott, A. (1982). A comparison of three treatment group formats for facilitating social interaction. Occupational Therapy in Mental Health 2(4): 1–16.

Slavson, S. R. (1950). Analytic Group Psychotherapy with Children, Adolescents and Adults. New York: Columbia University Press.

103

Tuckman, B. W. (1965). Developmental sequence in small groups. Psychological Bulletin 63: 384–399.

White, R. W. (1959). Motivation reconsidered: The concept of competence. The Psychological Review 66: 297–333.

White, R. W. (1971). The urge towards competence. American Journal of Occupational Therapy 25(6): 271–274.

Yalom, I. D. (1970). The Theory and Practice of Group Psychotherapy. New York: Basic Books.

Leadership and Four Stages of the Functional Group

The first part of this book deals primarily with definitions of groups, and descriptions of how they function. We examine occupational therapy group work from the perspective of history and of current practice. Finally, we present a functional model for group work.

In Part II, we consider the application of the functional group model to clinical practice. Chapter 5 is an overview of the issues and expectations concerning group leadership followed by an exploration of the skills required for effective group leadership and a discussion of intervention strategies intended to assist group leaders.

The leader can better assist the group to achieve its goals if the leader is aware of the stages of a group's development, of the inevitable critical events, and of the problems that are usually raised and solved. The

developmental stages through which a group must travel do not always proceed in a predictable manner. The course is often marked with fluctuations. Stages may overlap, or the group may temporarily regress to earlier stages. A group may also stay on a plateau for a number of sessions before moving to a different level of function. An understanding of the patterns of change enables the leader to guide the group and to assist the members to mobilize their resources toward achieving both individual and group goals.

While patterns in the development of a group may often continue over a number of sessions, each individual group meeting will also display developmental characteristics. Each group meeting can be seen as a microcosm of a sequence of meetings. An individual group session will begin with a formation period, when members greet each other, establish the climate, and review or establish the goals and norms of the group. The session then proceeds to the working stage, and eventually enters the termination period. Short-term and open groups go through a developmental pattern in individual sessions, even though these developmental periods may be abbreviated and more superficial than in the long-term groups.

Chapters 6 through 9 follow the developmental sequence of groups from beginning to end. Chapter 6 introduces the first phase of the functional group, the design stage.

The issues and expectations typically found in the second, or formation, stage of the group, are discussed in Chapter 7. Chapter 8 presents the important issues and expectations of stage three, the development stage. Chapter 9 covers stage four, the termination stage. At each point, leader functions and intervention strategies are discussed. In addition, we introduce in Chapter 6 detailed case studies of two sample groups. We will follow these groups through each of the four stages in order to enable the reader to view the results of applying the functional group model.

5

Role of the Leader in the Functional Group

"Sometimes it is merely the offering of help which is therapeutic." (Rogers, 1967, p. 270)

Definitions of Leadership

Social scientists have long been interested in the subject of group leadership, and much research has been done on the topic. Researchers have been concerned with identifying characteristics that made individuals effective group leaders. In approaching this issue, social scientists accepted a number of diverse assumptions about leadership; consequently, their studies led them in different directions. In the following pages we will discuss four attempts to define leadership.

Personality Traits

For many years, researchers viewed leadership as the combination of personality traits in a particular person. They studied particularly the traits that they felt a good leader should possess—intelligence, warmth, decisiveness, and assertiveness. This approach yielded little conclusive evidence. There were inevitably good leaders who were not decisive, not warm, or not assertive, even though these traits were found to be common among people who were judged to be effective leaders. This direction of inquiry also proved futile in identifying prospective leaders. Nevertheless, the research results did suggest, according to Stogdill (1948), "that leadership is a relation that exists between persons in a social situation, and that persons who are leaders in one situation may not necessarily be leaders in other situations" (p. 65).

Situations

When research into personality traits failed to provide conclusive data, social scientists turned to studying the circumstances in which leadership was present. They asked, do leaders emerge from a particular set of group circumstances? The hypothesis was that a leader's behavior in one setting may well differ from that of a second leader in a different setting. In addition, they postulated that the behavior of a leader might differ from one group situation to another. This course of inquiry was pursued by Homans (1950), who studied groups on a naval vessel during wartime. He found that leaders among these individuals changed according to the demands of the situation at hand. When there was little work to be done on board ship and groups faced inactivity and boredom, individuals who could be entertaining became popular and won recognition. When the ship came to port, those who had knowledge about the port, had been there before, or had contacts on land immediately became the leaders of the group. This study seems to emphasize that groups select leaders according to how well an individual's skill or knowledge meets the needs of the situation. Like the earlier emphasis on personality traits, the situation and timing implies that leadership is more a matter of chance than a skill that can be learned and developed.

Behaviors

A different approach to the study of leadership was conceived by Kurt Lewin and his associates (Lewin, Lippitt, and White, 1939), who examined the effects that different leadership behaviors have on groups of ten-year-old boys in a summer day camp. The experiment studied three different leadership styles: autocratic, democratic, and laissez-faire. Group leaders were trained to assume these different leadership styles. In the autocratic group, the decision-making power was under the control of the designated leader. In the democratic group, the decision-making power was in the control of the group but under the guidance of the leader, and in the laissez-faire group, the decision-making power was left entirely to the individuals in the group.

The autocratic leader dictated rules to be followed and did not discuss problems with the children. He did not participate in the group except when giving instructions and demonstrating how the instructions should be followed. Under democratic leadership, all policies were open for discussion and decision by the group. The leader helped the group to build a decision-making process of its own. The leader acted as a resource person for the group. The laissez-faire leader presented the group members with the supplies that they needed for their work and gave them information when asked. Otherwise, this leader took no part in the group. Lewin reached five conclusions after evaluating these three groups.

1. The democratic leadership style resulted in a more satisfying, efficient leadership than did the laissez-faire.
2. Autocratic leadership resulted in a slightly higher group productivity than did the other two leadership styles, but showed a significantly poorer quality of work than did the group with democratic leadership.

3. The autocratic leadership style created hostility and aggression in the group members.
4. There was greater dependency and less individuality in the autocratically led group than in the democratic group.
5. There was a greater degree of group cohesiveness, sense of comradeship, and high morale in the democratic group than in either of the other two groups.

These studies were published by Lewin, Lippitt and White (1939) and have now become classic. The results show clearly that different patterns of leadership result in different kinds of behavior among members of a group.

Functions

According to another group of researchers, leadership functions are directly related to group functions. Leadership is viewed as the ability to promote those behaviors that lead to the satisfaction of group needs. There are two categories of leadership function. The first relates to the achievement of the group goals or tasks, and is called the *task function.* The second relates to helping the group build and maintain a processs that enables the group to strengthen itself. This is called the *maintenance function.* In successful groups both functions are part of the ongoing life of the group. Group behavior may address both of these functions simultaneously, but frequently one function is served at the expense of the other. For example, a group may be so intent on reaching the task goal that it does not strengthen its decision-making process and depends on one individual (perhaps the leader) to make all decisions. In this case, the group is putting its efforts into task functions while neglecting its maintenance functions. The relative importance of group building (maintenance) and goal achievement (task) for any group may change dramatically from the early meetings to the later stages of development.

In most group situations, one person is designated the leader. The leader needs to share leadership responsibility with the members, so that they can learn both maintenance and task functions. Lippitt developed a list of ways in which the group leader can increase the effectiveness of the group (1961, p. 35):

1. At the beginning of any group's life, help the group to come to a clear understanding of the goals that it wants to reach

2. Help the group become aware of its own procedures
3. Help the group understand the skills, talents, and resources within its own membership
4. Help the group develop group methods of evaluation so that both leader and members can find ways of improving their procedures
5. Help the group to learn to accept new ideas and members without conflict
6. Assist the group in creating new tasks and in terminating outdated ones

Many of the suggestions presented by Lippitt strongly resemble the conduct found in the democratic leadership style. The role of the leader is to develop and support the processes within the group that enable it to grow and to take on greater responsibility for making its own decisions and for reaching its own goals.

Our understanding of the group leader's role has changed over time, and will continue to change as research and practical experience modify our views of leadership. As leaders of functional groups, we understand the leader to be in a dynamic relationship with the members. In this context, the emphasis is on what actions are required by the group members, under various conditions, if they are to achieve their goals, and on how group members can best take part in these actions. When leadership is defined in terms of behaviors that further the goals of the group, it becomes difficult to separate leadership roles from membership roles. Groups with a highly structured leader-centered process will have low membership involvement. Groups with an emphasis on membership involvement will have less leadership involvement. Tannenbaum and Schmidt (1958) identified the range of possible leader and member involvement on a continuum ranging from leader-centered leadership to group-centered leadership (Fig. 5-1).

The theory that leadership varies according to the leader's interaction with the group is congruent with the model for the functional group in occupational therapy. This concept of leadership encourages the would-be leader to develop the skills necessary for active participation in group functions and the ability to assume a variety of leadership roles. Interpersonal effectiveness is a measure of the degree to which one's leadership behavior matches one's intended role as group leader.

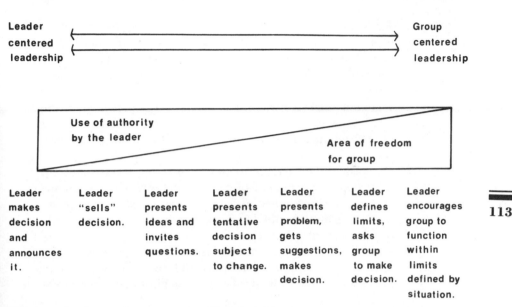

FIG. 5-1. Leader-member continuum. (Modified from Tannenbaum, R., and Schmidt, W. H. (1958). How to choose a leadership pattern. Harvard Business Review 36 (March-April):96)

Leadership Skills

Planning the Group Activity

The group leader is responsible for planning the activity of the functional group. In the early sessions of a closed or ongoing group, the leader must select the group task and decide the length, number, and types of tasks in each meeting. In addition, as soon as possible the leader must begin involving members in selecting a task and teaching members to assist in formulating and adapting the goals of the group's activity.

In the process of choosing an activity, the leader relies on his or her professional knowledge of activities. Hopkins, Smith and Tiffany (1983) have published guidelines on selecting occupational therapy activities for individual patients, and these guidelines can be applied to functional groups. In selecting a group activity, the leader must bear in mind four main points:

1. The goals of the activity should have meaning for the group members. The meaning of any activity will vary, depending upon the stages of development of the group. The activity should be useful to individual members and related to their interests and roles.
2. The group members should be able to participate in choosing or adapting the given activity, thus assuring a minimum level of self-initiated mental or physical participation in the process.
3. The task should enable members to take an active role in the group. They should be interested in the task; the demands of the task should elicit an adaptive response, and the members' response should be supported by its organization at the subcortical level.
4. The activity should be adaptable and gradable according to member skills, ages, or performance levels. This includes an awareness of the individual's relationship to and role in the group.

The task is a crucial factor in the treatment of individuals in a functional group. The task may be recreational, physical, academic, or vocational, but regardless of its nature, the task must facilitate the attainment of group goals as well as of individual treatment goals. Group discussion is an activity common to practically all group meetings, but the leader, in consultation with the group, must decide how much time is to be spent in discussion and how much is to be spent on the task itself.

Members of therapy groups often have a limited repertoire of social skills and interests. In the past, they may have often met with failure when attempting new tasks and this failure tended to discourage their involvement in new experiences. Because of this tendency, the group leader must plan not only the activity but also stimulate member interest in the task.

Genuineness and Empathy

A genuine person is one who can be himself or herself while interacting with other people and maintain an openness to the feelings and attitudes that are experienced. This general principle applies to a group leader. The term *genuineness* implies an ability to share intimate feelings when appropriate. The leader is conscious of the feelings he or she is experiencing and is able to communicate them to the group members, if desired. In studying therapy groups, Galigor (1977) found that group members who view their leader as "open, accepting, responsive and confident" did not drop out of the groups as readily as did those members who saw their leader as "distant, neutral or professional."

Egan (1975) identifies two characteristics of the genuine person. The first is spontaneity; the genuine person is able to communicate easily about immediate events without being impulsive. When the leader reflects on what has been said in the group, he or she is motivated by a concern for the group members, not by self-protection. The second characteristic of the genuine person is non-defensiveness. "The genuine person is non-defensive. He has a feeling for his areas of strength and his areas of deficit in living and presumably is trying to live more effectively all the time. When a client expresses negative attitudes toward him, he tries to understand what the client is thinking and feeling, and he continues to work with him" (p. 92).

Empathy, often explained as caring for and understanding another individual, is another skill of the effective group leader. In a factor analysis of the attributes of good leaders, Lieberman, Yalom and Miles (1973) found that the most effective leaders were rated high in caring. They defined caring as a leadership style that offered members protection, friendship, and affection. Caring leaders provided frequent opportunities for members to receive feedback as well as praise and encouragement for their behavior. Another quality of caring was careful listening and attending to what was being expressed in the group. Members are reassured when the speaker identifies himself with the listener's problems and accepts the other person's emotional reactions at face value. Communication that conveys respect for the listener is supportive and reduces the defensiveness of the listener. Gestures and other behavioral signs are also important in communicating empathy and caring.

Modeling Behavior

In Chapter 1 we discussed how the structure of the group helps to establish the legitimate group norms, values, and limits of behavior. The group leader has a role in this process, particularly in the early stages of the group. The leader is viewed as the central person or spokesperson of the group and his overt behavior strengthens the norms and values of the group. The functional group leader helps members learn new behaviors that will increase their ability to meet group needs and personal goals. This learning process can occur in a number of different ways, through direct instruction, through group experiences, or through a combination of both.

The studies of Lieberman, Yalom and Miles (1973) found that effective group leaders were characterized by "meaning attribution." The term *meaning attribution* refers to the tendency of the group leader to clarify, explain, understand and interpret what is happening in the group. These points in a discussion give members a framework for change. The authors found that effective leaders spent time in their groups explaining to the members why they did what they did and why they structured the group in a particular way. They also shared with the group their perceptions of how members interacted with each other at specific moments during the group session. Napier and Gershenfeld (1973) also support the importance of meaning attribution to group learning. They comment, "Learning is more likely to be retained and internalized in an atmosphere in which leaders (or other members) clarify what they or others are doing" (p. 34).

A second approach to teaching new skills is through the modeling of the desired behaviors. The imitation of leader behavior is followed by a positive reinforcement of group members through recognition and approval. According to the social learning theory of Bandura (1969), this is a valuable method for learning and teaching new skills. In order to teach group members through modeling, leaders must first learn themselves the behavior that they hope members will learn as part of their group experience. Johnson (1972) writes, "The word modeling refers to the process by which one person engages in ideal behavior to serve as an example to be imitated by other persons. If you, for example, engage in self-disclosure and the other person imitates you by also engaging in self-disclosure, a modeling process has taken place" (p. 189).

A group member who is relatively unskilled in interpersonal relations may learn interpersonal skills by observing the leader-model. If a group member is brought to note the consequences of any particular behavior, the member will see that positive results can be achieved by adapting his particular mode of conduct. In another instance, a member may know a certain mode of behavior but not know when to apply it; the leader can guide the member in discovering the correct circumstances for certain modes of behavior. In perhaps the most common scenario, a group member simply watches and copies the leader's behavior. For this reason, leaders must carefully consider the modes of conduct and the responses they will elicit from the group.

According to Johnson (1972), a leader must understand the following aspects of the modeling process in order to teach a certain mode of behavior effectively:

1. You must have the attention of the other person. If the other person is not aware of your behavior, he or she cannot imitate it.
2. If others think that imitating your behavior will help them to accomplish their own goals, they will be apt to imitate your behavior.
3. If imitating leader behavior brought success in the past, there is a stronger possibility that leader behavior will be imitated in the present.
4. If other people value your friendship, like you, or seek your approval, they are more likely to imitate your behavior.
5. People are more likely to imitate your behavior when they are emotionally aroused.
6. If another person is unsure about what behavior is appropriate in a given situation and you are not unsure, that person will tend to imitate you.

Leaders who wish to help a member develop interpersonal skills must demonstrate those skills in the group. Further, they must develop a group climate that is supportive and accepting so that members will dare to try new behaviors in the group. Group members make the most progress in a group in which they feel comfortable and are encouraged to explore new possibilities.

Reality Testing

The effective leader also assists the group to achieve its goals through reality testing. Because of its focus on a task and on the relationship between thinking and feeling, the functional group provides an excellent milieu for learning new behaviors. The shared reality that is part of each group meeting creates opportunities for testing reality. Further, because of its norms and its support for honest expression, the group offers ample opportunities for consensual validation. Consensual validation is achieved through a comparison of one's own interpersonal evaluations with those of others in the group. Here perceptions can be tested and discussed. Here behavior can be altered or reinforced according to its relation to reality. Recording the group session on audio or video tape and replaying the tapes in the group can enhance reality testing.

In a list of curative factors present in therapy groups, Yalom (1970) places reality testing near the top of the list. Similarly, Carl Rogers (1959) includes reality testing among patient behaviors that reflect a good therapeutic relationship.

In addition to assisting members to test the reality of their behaviors, the leader should test the reality of his or her behavior within the group. Leaders often become the target of members' conflictual behaviors regarding persons in authority. This involves a phenomenon called transference. In *transference*, the member finds in the leader certain qualities associated with past figures of authority. Usually the leader does not actually possess these qualities. The effective leader can counter these inaccurate perceptions through reality testing, and can do much to clarify a member's perception of the leader as an individual.

Communicating

The interpersonal effectiveness of the leader depends upon his or her ability to communicate clearly, to create the desired impression, to influence another person in a specific manner. Interpersonal effectiveness can be improved through several techniques, including self-disclosure, feedback on behavior, and adjusting behavior until other individuals perceive it as it was intended. In this section we will discuss five of the most commonly used communication skills.

Listening and responding. The way you listen and respond to another person is crucial for building a positive relationship. Through the way you listen and respond, you can make the relationship either a distant one or a close, more personal one. In a close relationship it is important to let the other person know that you have heard and understood what was said to you.

According to Johnson (1972), one of the major barriers to building close relationships is the tendency to judge, evaluate, approve, or disapprove of a statement that has been made to you. "This happens when the sender makes a statement and you respond internally or openly with, 'I think you're wrong,' 'I don't like what you said,' 'I think your views are right,' or 'I agree entirely.' " (p. 75). People tend to respond with evaluative statements when strong feelings are involved. The stronger the feelings, the more likely that those involved will evaluate the statements according to their own points of view.

Learning to be a good listener is an important skill for every group leader. It takes considerable effort and practice to learn to listen accurately. Below are four suggestions for improving listening skills:

1. Make a firm commitment to listen.
2. Get physically ready to listen and attend.
3. Dismiss other concerns from your mind. Concentrate on the other person as a communicator.
4. Give the person a full hearing, avoiding interruption unless absolutely necessary. Impatience can lead to false understanding.

Feedback.   Stating your reaction to another person's behavior is called feedback. The purpose of this technique is to help other people become aware of how you perceive their behavior and of how their behavior affects you. Feedback enables people to improve performance in achieving their desired goals.

Feedback should be given in a manner that is not threatening to the other person. The more defensive the individuals are, the less likely they will correctly hear and understand your remarks. People need both positive and negative feedback. They need to know not only what is ineffective, but also what is effective so that they can correct the one and continue the other. Feedback is most successfully communicated when a relationship of trust and confidence has been established in the group.

Timing is important in giving and receiving feedback. It is generally most helpful if it is connected with a specific incident, that is, if it can be given in terms of objective data that have just been observed in the group. This gives the recipient of the feedback the opportunity to compare it with the reactions or observations of the other members in the group. Sometimes it is unwise to give feedback right after the incident in question, particularly if strong feelings have been aroused and people need time to calm down. Negative feedback is often viewed as criticism, and people react to it by defending themselves through rationalization, denial, or suspicion of the motives of the person giving the feedback. Therefore, a leader or member should exercise discretion when giving negative feedback.

Feedback can be given to a group as well as to individuals. Like individuals, a group can benefit from receiving information about its performance. The group may need to know that the atomosphere is defensive, that members are having difficulty being heard, or that there is too much reliance on the leader. The general guidelines for individual feedback also apply to group feedback. The group may receive feedback from members acting as participant observers or leaders. Forms and questionnaires may be used to elicit feedback.

Concreteness.   In some groups, vagueness and superficiality can become a serious problem, leading members to avoid talking about specific issues. The leader can help the group move toward its goals by using concrete language to communicate with the group. If leaders use concrete examples in their communications with the group members, the members, by imitation, will learn to focus on concrete behaviors in their explorations of their own behavior patterns. Learning to be concrete can be particularly helpful to members of functional groups in which avoidance and reality contact have been identified as problems for certain members.

Successful problem solving requires becoming progressively more concrete. When a group is involved in problem-solving tasks, a problem concretely stated can more easily be translated into achieved goals. If goals are stated in concrete terms, members can begin to define the means needed to reach those goals. Further, concrete goals can be broken down into smaller, more easily achieved subunits. Finally, concreteness can be effectively used to reduce ambiguity, and when ambiguity is lessened, the anxiety of group members is also lessened.

Confrontation.   Johnson (1972) defines confrontation as "a deliberate attempt to help another person examine the consequences of some aspect of his behavior. It is an invitation to self-examination." (p. 160). He continues, "A confrontation originates from a desire on the part of the confronter to involve himself more deeply with the person he is confronting. Confrontation is a way of expressing concern for another person and a wish to increase the mutual involvement in the relationship. The first rule of confrontation is, 'Do not confront another person if you do not intend to increase your involvement with him' " (p. 160).

The decision to confront another person is made on the basis of one's relationship with that person. The quality of the relationship is important; the stronger the relationship, the more powerful the confrontation will be. A leader must also consider the ability of the person being confronted to act upon the confrontation. If that person's motivation to change is low or if his or her anxiety level is high, the confrontation will probably be seen not as an invitation for self-examination, but as an attack. In this instance, a confrontation should not be initiated.

In their study of therapy groups, Lieberman, Yalom, and Miles (1973) found four attributes of effective leaders; among these was moderation in the area of emotional stimulation. By emotional stimulation, these authors meant behaviors that strongly encourage revealing feelings. Self-disclosure and confrontation may encourage, and sometimes coerce, members to go beyond a level that they feel is comfortable for them. This may cause members to withdraw or even to leave the group. Under most circumstances, confrontation is best approached tentatively and with qualifications that enable the member to accept the message, to add to it, or receive it without feeling accused by the leader. Confrontation is best done in a group that has achieved a high degree of trust and cohesiveness.

Self-disclosure. Letting another person know what you think, feel, or want is called *self-disclosure.* The term refers to revealing feelings about a present situation and giving information about the past that is relevant to an understanding of how you experience the present. Leaders who practice self-disclosure are more easily seen by members as real people rather than as impersonal leaders. Members get to know and understand leaders not through their past history but through knowing how they react. The past history is only helpful if it clarifies why the leader is reacting in a particular way. Engaging in self-disclosure means taking a risk of being misunderstood or rejected; therefore, in responding to another person's self-disclosure, it is important to be accepting and supportive. Jourard (1964) has studied self-disclosure extensively. He reports that women seem to find self-disclosure easier than males, and that some cultural groups are more prone to self-disclosure than others.

Leadership Strategies

The several leadership skills described above enable the leader of a group to guide members in their efforts to achieve specific goals. In addition to employing specific leadership skills, a leader may use strategies designed to gather information from an entire group. Each strategy uses the same three-step process. First, the leader collects data about the group. Second, the leader reports the data to the group. Finally, the group defines the problem indicated by the data and designs a solution. Bradford, Stock, and Horwitz (1978) insist that both members and leaders, that is, the entire group, must collaborate in all parts of this process. In the functional group, the leader is responsible for teaching group members how to participate in procedures. As observers and resource persons, the leaders can offer to the group for discussion specific concerns gathered from observation, analysis, and experience.

A leader can also teach group members to assume some of the data-gathering functions. Leaders can use several techniques for gathering observations about a group's verbal and nonverbal behavior. Several of these are described below and can be used in conjunction with the leadership skills already discussed.

Methods of Observation

Sociogram. A sociogram is an instrument that provides data on a communication pattern in the group. It charts specifically who talks to whom. By using this technique, the observer can follow the flow of the conversation and identify members who speak often, members who speak seldom, and members who are the recipients of comments or questions.

To use a sociogram, the leader draws a circle and marks the members of the group by name in their places in the circle (see Fig. 5-2). The leader then draws a line for each statement or question, indicating the initiator and the recipient. A sociogram usually records the number of statements made during a 10-minute period. Some lines may extend only to the center of the circle; these represent statements that were made to the group as a whole and that were not directed toward a specific individual. The arrows at both ends of the line indicate that the statement made by one person to the other was responded to by the recipient. In the sample in Figure 5-2, Bruce received more statements than anyone else. Mary spoke to two persons, but no one responded to her or addressed a statement

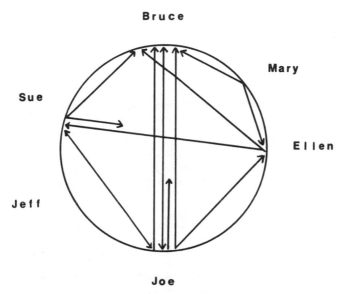

Bruce

Mary

Sue

Ellen

Jeff

Joe

FIG. 5-2. Sociogram.

to her. Although 15 statements were made during that 10-minute period, Jeff was not involved in any of these communications.

Sociograms are commonly used at intervals during the course of a group meeting. Schwartzberg, Howe, and McDermott (1982) report doing a sociogram for 5 minutes at two different points in the group session, at 20 minutes and again at 40 minutes after the beginning of the group session, to gather research data on group communication.

Sociograms are also useful in identifying group members' communication patterns. For instance, a sociogram may reveal that some group members talked only to the leader, perhaps indicating their dependence upon the leader and their reluctance or inability to get involved with the other group members.

Interaction process analysis. Bales (1950) developed a method for analyzing verbal interactions made during a group meeting (see Fig. 5-3). His system for observing and recording is based on his theory regarding the two main points of group process: task issues and maintenance issues. Bales sought to distinguish between communications that give information and those that seek information.

124

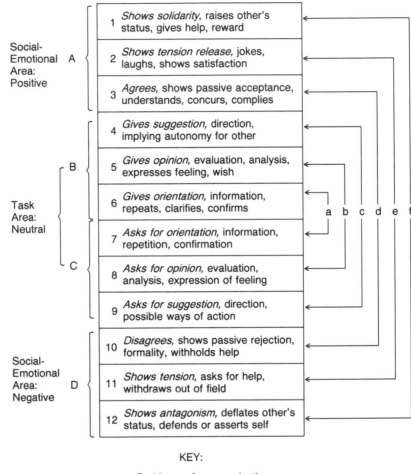

KEY:

a Problems of communication
b Problems of evaluation
c Problems of control
d Problems of decision
e Problems of tension reduction
f Problems of reintegration

A Positive reactions
B Attempted answers
C Questions
D Negative reactions

FIG. 5-3. Bales interaction process analysis chart. (From Bales, R. (1950). Interaction process analysis. Reading, MA: Addison Wesley, p. 59. Copyright 1950 by The University of Chicago.)

He also differentiated between emotionally negative and positive expressions and between behavior and verbal content. This system of communication analysis can be added to the sociogram by marking the lines of the sociogram with letters keyed to Bales's categories, thereby recording both who talks to whom and the types of communications made.

Member role observation.   Leaders may also gather information from group observation by completing a member role form (Fig 5-4). The members' names are placed at the top of the form and a check mark is placed in the column corresponding to the role that the member plays most often in the group. By filling out this form, leaders can quickly arrive at a rating of the different types of roles that were assumed by the participants in the group. This form also allows the observer to note any important roles that were not assumed by group members. If the leader-observer wants to record frequency of roles adopted, he can place a check in the column every time that the designated member has assumed that particular role in the group. The various member roles are defined in Chapter 1.

Content and process analysis.   An analysis of the content and process of a group session provides a basis for an evaluation of a group meeting. This procedure may be used by group leaders for their own analysis or by all group members for evaluation and discussion. The leader or member or both should answer specific questions on content and process (see Fig. 5-5), and a follow-up discussion should be focused on the ensuing information.

Analysis of group behavior.   The leader can gain an understanding of group behavior by making observations of the nonverbal behavior of the members. Nonverbal communication, such as touching or gesturing while talking or listening, is frequently seen in a group, and can reveal how members feel about each other. Posture indicating inclusion or withdrawal is another form of nonverbal communication. For example, a member may lean toward the circle of members, or away from them. Similarly, posture indicates interest and attention or boredom. If members of the group are sitting far apart from each other, this indicates that certain individuals feel isolated in the group. Eye contact and eye language may signal intimacy or confrontation and avoidance of eye contact may mean reluctance to get involved. Sweeping eye contact often indicates a search for support or feedback.

ROLES	MEMBER NAMES							
TASK ROLES								
Initiator								
Information/Opinion Giver								
Information/Opinion Seeker								
Energizer								
Coordinator								
Recorder								
MAINTENANCE ROLES								
Encourager								
Harmonizer/Compromiser								
Gatekeeper								
Standard Setter								
Follower								
INDIVIDUAL ROLES								
Playboy								
Blocker								
Dominator								
Recognition Seeker								

FIG. 5-4. Member role evaluation form.

Other types of member behavior can communicate meaning in the group. No behavior is random or accidental. Such things as eating, smoking, drinking, or visits to the bathroom can be gauges of the level of tension or boredom in the group. Periods of silence also have meanings. Observing how people look during periods of

Content Observations:

1. What were the main ideas presented in the discussion?
2. Which ideas were accepted?
3. Were there irrelevant ideas and discussion presented?
4. Did the group have the information necessary for making decisions?
5. Did the members talk about ideas and facts or feelings?

Process Observations:

1. Describe the tone of the discussion (e.g., friendly, tense, angry, anxious).
2. Is the atmosphere conducive to free expression? Why?
3. Identify any communication blocks (e.g., some members were not listened to; some were not understood; some were not recognized).
4. What factors seemed to keep the group from functioning well? (e.g., some members were uncomfortable; some couldn't hear because it was noisy; some seemed bored; and some came late. The group was not organized to do the job it was trying to do.)
5. What factors assisted the group's function?
6. Were there any indications of dissatisfaction with the kinds of decisions that were made by the group?

FIG. 5-5. Content and process analysis.

silence—sad, tense, contemplative—gives the leader clues about the members' feelings.

Meeting evaluations.   Leaders can ask members to evaluate meetings at the end of a session by completing evaluation forms. Howe (1968) reported the use of a brief rating form through which group members anonymously provide feedback in an occupational therapy activity group. On these forms, members checked whether they felt that the meeting was good, fair, or poor, and whether they were able to express these feelings to the group. Knowles (1970) suggested an expanded evaluation form, which he calls an end of the meeting form (Fig. 5-6). The design of this form allows members to make any comments they choose while also asking them to focus on the session just completed.

Conclusion

128

The leader of any group is responsible for assisting the group members to achieve their stated goals. Although the definition of a leader is still being debated, research has developed several techniques that aid leaders in carrying out their roles. Not all of these strategies or techniques will be suitable for every leader and every group. Some leaders will be most comfortable using communication skills reinforced by the results of a sociogram; other leaders may find the evaluation forms especially valuable. Still other leaders may find that the behavior of the group calls for modifications of these strategies. Each skill and each strategy must be adapted to suit the needs of the group.

Date: Activity:
Please circle the phrase that best describes how you feel.

1. I think that in this meeting I learned
   a great deal   quite a lot   some   very little   nothing
2. On the whole, today's session was
   excellent   pretty good   all right   disappointing   terrible
3. I am leaving the meeting feeling
   enthusiastic   encouraged   all right   disappointed   frustrated
4. At this time, this activity interests me
   immensely   quite a bit   somewhat   a little   not at all

Comments: _____

_____

_____

FIG. 5-6. Meeting evaluation form. (Adapted from Knowles, M. S. (1970). The modern practice of adult education. New York: Association Press, p. 233)

References

Bandura, A. (1969). Principles of Behavior Modification. New York: Holt Reinhart & Winston.

Bales, R. (1950). Interaction Process Analysis. Reading, MA: Addison Wesley.

Bradford, L., Stock, D., and Horwitz, M. (1978). How to diagnose group problems. In L. Bradford (ed.), Group Development (2nd ed.). La Jolla, CA: University Associates.

Egan, G. (1975). The Skilled Helper. Monterey, CA: Brooks/Cole.

Galigor, J. (1977). Perceptions of the group therapist and the dropout from group. In A. R. Wolberg and M. L. Aronson (eds.), Group Therapy 1977: An Overview. New York: Stratton Intercontinental Medical Book Corporation.

Homans, G. (1950). The Human Group. New York: Harcourt, Brace.

Hopkins, H., Smith, H., and Tiffany, E. G. (1983). Therapeutic application of activity. In H. Hopkins and H. Smith (eds.), Willard and Spackman's Occupational Therapy (6th ed.). Philadelphia: J. B. Lippincott.

Howe, M. C. (1968). An occupational therapy activity group. American Journal of Occupational Therapy 22(3): 176–179.

Johnson, D. W. (1972). Reaching Out: Interpersonal Effectiveness and Self-actualization. Englewood Cliffs, NJ: Prentice-Hall.

Jourard, S. (1964). The Transparent Self. Princeton: Van Nostrand Company.

Knowles, M. S. (1970). The Modern Practice of Adult Education. New York: Association Press.

Lewin, K., Lippitt, R., and White, R. (1939). Patterns of aggressive behavior in experimentally created social climates. Journal of Social Psychology 10: 271–299.

Lieberman, M., Yalom, I., and Miles, M. (1973). Encounter Groups: First Facts. New York: Basic Books.

Lippitt, G. L. (1961). How to get results from a group. In L. P. Bradford (ed.), Group Development. La Jolla, CA: University Associates.

Napier, N., and Gershenfeld, M. (1973). Groups: Theory and Experience. Boston: Houghton Mifflin.

Rogers, C. (1959). Theory of therapy-personality and interpersonal relationships. In S. Koch (ed.), Psychology: A Study of a Science (vol. 3). New York: McGraw-Hill.

Rogers, C. (1967). The process of the basic encounter group. In J. Bugental (ed.), Challenges of Humanistic Psychology. New York: McGraw-Hill.

Schwartzberg, S., Howe, M., and McDermott, A. (1982). A comparison of three treatment group formats for facilitating social interaction.

Occupational Therapy in Mental Health: A Journal for Psychosocial Practice and Research 2(4): 1–16.

Stogdill, R. M. (1948). Personality factors associated with leadership: A survey of the literature. Journal of Psychology 25: 3–71.

Tannenbaum, R., and Schmidt, W. H. (1958). How to choose a leadership pattern. Harvard Business Review 36 (March-April): 95–101.

Yalom, I. (1970). The Theory and Practice of Group Psychotherapy. New York: Basic Books.

6

Stage 1: Design

The functional group is a procedure directed toward the use of time and energy in purposeful action in order to promote adaptation through occupation. Such groups progress through four successive, interdependent stages. These stages are design, formation, development, and termination.

The purpose of this chapter is to describe the leadership tasks of the design stage. Unlike the other stages, stage 1 involves only the group leader or co-leaders, and covers the leader's preparation prior to actual group formation and implementation. Although issues related to the other three stages may first arise in the design stage, those issues are not resolved at this point. The main purpose of the design stage is to establish the initial group structure for the next stage—the formation stage.

The specific leader functions of this stage are (1) assessing the need for a group, (2) determining group goals and methods, (3) developing a group plan, (4) selecting group members, and (5) structuring the group and its tasks. Beginning with this chapter, we shall follow two groups through the successive stages. These two groups are identified as Open Occupational Therapy Group–Case Study Number 1 and Closed Occupational Therapy Group–Case Study Number 2. In addition to the standard forms useful to the leader in this stage, we have included at the end of this chapter completed sample forms for the case studies.

Assessing the Need for a Group

The functional group is aimed at individuals who have experienced a physical injury or illness, suffer from an emotional, developmental, or congenital disorder, or have difficulty in dealing with the aging process and need assistance in adapting to their life situations. To eliminate any confusion about the focus of this group in light of the wide range of possible members, we shall further clarify the purpose of the group by stating what it is not. The functional group is *not*

> Restricted to particular settings, *e.g.*, inpatient or outpatient settings
> Aimed at treating the etiology of diseases
> Aimed at teaching components of skills in isolation
> Aimed at teaching isolated behaviors

Product-oriented; the goal is not a product alone

Focused solely on primary process, on developing insight, and delving into psychohistorical issues

Aimed at teaching a progression of age/stage-specific skills or behaviors

The specific types of approaches excluded above are the domain of other models; for instance, psychoanalytic groups are better prepared to delve into historical issues. The functional group focuses on aiding an individual's adaptation through purposeful, self-initiated, spontaneous, and group-centered activity.

To determine the suitability of a group membership for any individual, the leader usually conducts an initial needs assessment. The functional group would be an appropriate tool for an individual with the following needs:

1. Evaluating occupational behaviors necessary for functioning in life roles
2. Achieving the occupational behaviors prerequisite to successful functioning in life roles
3. Preventing deterioration of occupational behaviors necessary for adaptation
4. Facilitating the maintenance of health or state of adaptation

The needs listed here are broader than those listed in the categories of excluded needs given above. The emphasis here is on quality of functioning in a community rather than on mastering a given skill or resolving a specific problem.

Because of the broad nature of its goals, the functional group can be held in a variety of clinical settings. Occupational therapists see patients at a variety of points in the continuum of care. Depending upon the nature of the problem, the therapist may meet the prospective group member at an acute care section of a general hospital, in a spinal cord injury unit, rehabilitation hospital, nursing home, or in an outpatient facility, such as a school, day program, or partial hospitalization program that provides transitional or long-term care. Thus, prospective group members may have a variety of disorders, such as schizophrenia, borderline personality disorder, mental retardation, cerebrovascular accident, fracture, burn, spinal cord injury, or arthritis. The members can also be of varying ages, from a child to an older adult, and from a variety of socio-economic backgrounds.

The diversity of setting and population with which occupational therapists work offers a variety of opportunities for initiating functional groups. Nevertheless, the decision to offer a functional group depends in part upon an institution's aims and the roles and functions of the institution's health professionals. The professionals who deliver the services are generally not the same people who decide on the programs to be offered. In addition, patients' needs may not be the most significant factor in a decision. In discussing inpatient group psychotherapy, Yalom (1983) points out, "decisions about number, types, and frequency of groups are often made on the basis of what will not ruffle the staff rather than of what will be most effective for the patient" (p. 15). Funding also can play a role in determining the types of services offered. For many reasons occupational therapists rarely seek to work without a connection to an institutional setting—inpatient or community. Even therapists who conduct functional groups on a private practice basis usually work in collaboration with a referring physician or agency.

Because of their dependence on institutions and referring parties, occupational therapists must educate other professionals within these settings on the value of functional groups. When an occupational therapist identifies a community of individuals who might benefit from participation in a functional group, the therapist might present the initial report of a needs assessment as a tool to persuade those responsible for a final decision to consider offering a functional group program.

Screening mechanisms should be tailored to individual settings and populations. Therapists must determine if individuals need assistance in maintaining or developing occupational behaviors in order to function effectively in their life roles. They must also determine if a health maintenance program is needed within the institution. Specific methods of assessment have been devised and can be found in the occupational therapy literature (Barris, Kielhofner, and Watts, 1983; Hemphill, 1982; Mosey, 1973). In examining evaluation data, the therapist should ask several questions. Are there individuals who need help in order to effectively carry out and maintain their roles? Does this institution have a structure for maintaining health? Will this institution support the aims of a functional group? Finally, occupational therapists working in the well community must address one additional question. Does this environment maintain health and prevent deterioration of occupational behaviors necessary for human adaptation?

Determining Group Goals and Methods

After the leader has determined the need for a functional group, he or she must determine group goals and methods. In order for a group to be successful, group members should perceive the group as congruent with their needs and goals. The leader can determine the prospective member's goals through one of three techniques: pregroup interview, group history, and member assessment. Each technique is best suited to a particular circumstance; for example, the group history is designed for an institution that has an existing therapy group that will be changed to a functional group.

Pregroup Interview

The pregroup interview technique is designed to elicit the goals of prospective group members as well as inform the leader about the members in general. The leader can achieve several purposes with this interview: establish the member's level of functioning in occupational behaviors, self-perceived needs, and functional goals; form a beginning therapeutic rapport with the member; and explain the nature, expectations, and general purposes of a functional group.

On the basis of initial interviews the group leader tentatively outlines the group's general goals and methods prior to the initial meeting. This plan represents the starting point for the group and should be modified in an ongoing fashion as the group develops into a more cohesive unit. Ultimately, goal setting and program planning should be a collaborative process between group leaders and members as the group moves through successive stages.

Group History

If there is an established group, the leader can undertake a group history. This history should include answers to the questions shown on the Group History Form on page 137. The group history is usually constructed from the group's records rather than from interviewing members. It is important to include a clear statement of former and current goals of both individuals and the group as a whole. The group history can be used in conjunction with the third technique, assessment of members.

Group History Form

Name of Group_____
Date_____

1. How long has the group been in existence? What is its anticipated duration? What is its general stage and level of development? Who has authority over goals and structure of the group?

2. How was the group membership determined (voluntary or involuntary, etc.)?

3. How stable is the group membership? What is the rate of attendance? Is it an open or closed group? If it is an open group, are there any new members in the group? How long have the new and old members been in the group? If it is a closed group, what criteria were used to select members? How often and for how long a time did the group meet?

4. What is the existing group structure? Who has ultimate authority to change this structure?

5. What other factors, from the group's history, are pertinent to your understanding, assessing, and planning for the group (e.g., prior group leadership style)?

Member Assessment

If the occupational therapist has identified prospective members in a setting that allows the therapist to evaluate the individual's abilities in a wide range of areas, the therapist may choose to use a member assessment such as the one shown on pages 138–139. For example, a therapist in an inpatient institution could use this technique, but the leader of an open group in a setting outside a medical care institution would probably not. The assessment of members suggested here covers all facets of the member's health (diagnosis and treatment) and behavior (cognitive, psychosocial, neuro-motor, physical), as well as the member's general and specific goals. If possible, the leader or therapist should include an assessment of the member's performance and achievements to date.

In addition to the three techniques for collecting information on the possible goals of the group, the leader should consider the setting of the group and determine if the setting will influence the group's goals. The assessment should include the physical location, emotional environment, and administrative structure of the institution containing or sponsoring the group (see Assessment of Members Form on pp. 138–139).

Assessment of Members Form

1. Assessment of Group Members (Including *Range of Behaviors*)
   A. General description (include significant demographic and medical/psychological information)

   B. General description of members' expected environment (include specific information regarding where and with whom the group members will live and reside, as well as expected roles)

   C. Description of current performance in areas of occupational behavior
   Work:

   Self-care:

   Leisure:

   D. Cognitive behavior

   E. Psychosocial behavior

F. Physical and neuro-motor behavior

G. What is the significance of these factors with regard to individual member goals and forming or planning the group or group session(s)?

2. Assessment of Group Context (the Facility)
   A. General description of program in which group is included (administrative structure)

   B. General description of physical environment

   C. General description of emotional climate

   D. Frame of reference, purpose, and objectives

   E. What is the significance of these factors in forming or planning the group or group session(s)?

3. Assessment of Environmental Supports and Constraints
   A. Facilities and materials

   B. Scheduling

   C. Group norms and prior therapy group experience (if any)

   D. Do any of the environmental constraints require modification of the group, or could you alter the situation (such as locating needed materials)?

After the therapist has collected information on the members and their goals, he or she can distill from the many general and specific goals a set of goals that relate to all group members. For the sake of clarity, the goals should be stated in behavioral terms, although the functional group does not have a behavioral frame of reference. The leader should state the general behavioral goals for the client group (behaviors that are to be increased or decreased). Since setting goals is a continuing process usually done in conjunction with the members, the leader's initial goals may change over time. The therapist should also state in behavioral terms the criteria for successful attainment of goals in each session. As Yalom (1983) has clearly stated, "appropriate goal setting is of crucial importance to the proper functioning of the small therapy group. Overly ambitious goals impair the effectiveness of the group and lower the morale of the therapist" (p. 62).

Depending on the goals, the therapist should select a methodology. This might include activities such as structured exercises or the task of identifying the activity to be undertaken by the group. The methodology should suit the group's general goals, time frame, and structure. Like group goals, methods should be regularly adjusted to the pace of the group and its development.

Developing a Group Plan

After the leader establishes general goals and methods of the group, he or she should develop a general group plan, which provides the leader with a structure or cognitive strategy for interactions with the group. It should also serve as a guide for program planning while keeping the group working toward its goals. In all circumstances the leader needs a specific format, but this is especially true for open groups and acute care settings. In these circumstances the leader might have only one contact with a group member; consequently, each session must have optimal impact. The general group plan should be made available to all staff involved in the care of a group member.

In addition to a general group plan for the overall group structure, the therapist should develop a group session plan for each session. A *session evaluation form* is used to review the group's progress and to aid in reformulating the group session plan.

General Group Plan

The general group plan sets forth the overall framework for the group, from formation through termination. The plan presents a detailed statement of goals; criteria for achieving the goals; criteria for selecting group members, leadership roles, and functions; requirements for group members; and selected group methods and procedures, techniques, and strategies (see the General Group Plan Protocol below and that for Case Study No. 2). The goals presented are long-term and represent what should be achieved at the group's termination

---

General Group Plan Protocol

A. Name of Group_____

B. Time/length of meeting(s)_____

C. Place_____

D. Open_____or closed group_____
   Statement of rationale:

E. Group goals:
   Depending on the specific group, these may include primary and secondary objectives and leader objectives for group as a whole and/or individual members.
   1. Goals (*behaviors* you wish to increase or decrease)

   2. Rationale for goal selection

   3. Outcome criteria for successful goal attainment in session(s) stated in *behavioral* terms

F. Group composition or criteria for selecting members

G. Leadership roles and functions

H. Characteristics of group contract

I. Group methods and procedures to be employed: Briefly describe or list methods, techniques, and modalities

---

(closed group) or at an individual member's departure from the group (open group). The methods listed are procedural guides for planning and implementing specific techniques and modalities for achieving group goals. Because of its detail, the general plan is usually based on a group history or assessment of members. If these methods of assessment are not possible, initial group sessions may focus on member assessment and evaluation in order to develop a detailed general group plan.

Group Session Plan

142

The group session plan establishes the specific framework for one session (or unit of sessions) designed to partially fulfill a specific aspect of the general group plan. Goals are short-term and indicate the anticipated group achievement for the specific session or unit. The session plan also includes specific techniques and modalities for the session or unit (see below).

Group Session Plan Protocol

A. Name of Group_____
   Date_____
B. Specific goals for the group session
C. Specific goals for group members if different from above, and goals for each group member
D. Description of and rationale for methods and procedures
E. Description of and rationale for leadership role
F. Describe necessary preparations
G. List material and equipment needed
H. Time and sequence outline for sessions, including what you will do and say as leader, and what the group will do; consider both content and process.
I. Other information pertinent to this specific session: For example—will there be any new members, co-leaders, or guests; is there an unusual tone on the unit or special event that is about to occur or just occurred for the individual member or group?

Session Evaluation Form

As the group moves through its periods of development, the leader should evaluate the progress of the group and its members. A sample session evaluation form is presented on pages 143–144 as a guide to assist the leader in evaluating the group's progress toward long-term and short-term goals. The leader may also gather information on whether or not the selected techniques and modalities are appropriate for the group and on the effect of his own leadership behavior on the group. Changes are made according to the evaluations. The data collected can also be used to modify the general group plan and, later, group session plans.

Session Evaluation Form Protocol

A. Name of Group_____
   Date_____

B. Were the goals accomplished? (Give rationale and state outcome.)

   Was the session helpful in accomplishing short- and long-term group and individual member goals?

   Do you have any evidence that the session(s) have been helpful to the members' functioning (adaptation) outside of the group?

C. Was the group structure adequate for accomplishing the goals? Give rationale, and consider: leadership; time/length of meeting; open vs. closed group; time, sequence, methods and procedures; media/modalities/techniques employed; norms/behaviors reinforced implicitly or explicitly; methods of reinforcement; and stage of group's development.

   Did the structure provide optimal "action" or "flow activity" for a "flow state" to occur?

Did the structure provide optimal purposeful, self-initiated, spontaneous, and group-centered "action" for cognitive and emotional impact, skill learning, and adaptation to occur through "occupation"?

Did the structure provide for new learning, reinforcement of current level of functioning or adaptation, or did it reinforce functioning below current level of adaptation? Explain and give rationale.

Did the structure provide an opportunity for evaluation and feedback regarding the group procedures and member progress? Explain.

D. What changes would you make regarding group goals and structure for the next session, or if you were to lead this session again?

E. Were you adequately prepared for the session? (Give rationale, considering such things as time, place, materials, and physical and emotional environment.)

F. How did you function as leader? How did your behavior and role affect the group? Were you effective? (Give rationale.) What did you learn about yourself as group leader?

G. Was the group interaction as you anticipated? If problems occurred, what processes can you identify as a basis for understanding the problems?

H. In the future, what might you do differently as group leader? (Give rationale.)

Selecting Group Members

The functional group is open to anyone who has a physical injury or illness, an emotional, developmental, or congenital disorder, or difficulty coping with the aging process or changes in the environment. This description includes the elderly and adolescents. The group is also open to individuals who need a structure in order to maintain adaptation or to prevent deterioration of occupational behavior and adaptive skills.

Despite the broad description of individuals suitable for the functional group, not everyone can benefit from this format. According to Yalom (1983),

> There is considerable consensus in the research literature that psychotic patients are most successfully treated in supportive, reality-focused, structured group therapy and require a sealing over rather than an opening up. . . . They are made more anxious by an unstructured group experience and do less well in groups if they disclose a great deal about themselves. . . . An extensive review of the entire clinical literature reaches the same conclusion: psychotic patients do far better in in-patient therapy groups that are reality- or activity-oriented rather than in insight-oriented ones. . . . A review of group therapy in day treatment centers yields the identical conclusion: group therapy aimed at insight and derepression is contraindicated for the schizophrenic patient. . . . (p. 32)

Depending on the nature of the particular group, psychotic patients need not necessarily be excluded. The group can be oriented so that it is highly supportive. Further, the aim of the functional group is *not* insight or the examination of unconscious material alone. Indeed, the functional group is clearly reality-oriented.

Since peer groups play an important part in the normal development of adolescents, the functional group is particularly well suited to this age group. Adolescents need strong peer support to feel adequate as people. They are also developing a sense of self or personal identity and competency through testing a variety of behaviors. The activity and action orientation of the functional group match the modes of expression most often used by adolescents to explore their questions of identity and growth.

The wide range of individuals who are suited to the functional group indicates that the essential criteria qualifying an individual for the group are broad. There are five general criteria for the group member. Each member should be able to do the following:

1. Communicate verbally, in a simple manner
2. Understand simple communications, such as instructions (written or verbal)
3. Be able to focus on a structured task in the presence of two other group members, for a minimum of 30 minutes
4. Understand the purpose and nature of the group and the roles of the members and leader
5. Tolerate the stimulation of interpersonal contact

After considering an individual's general qualifications for membership, the leader must consider other factors. The group must be formed so that members work together in reasonable order. The number of possible members is therefore limited, as is the range of problems and goals that can be dealt with. In forming a particular group, the therapist must next consider composition and size.

Group Composition

A leader can determine the composition of a group according to one of three techniques. First, the leader can select members who are alike, who have similar adaptation problems or needs. The leader can look for similarity in skill deficit, role disorder, developmental disability, illness or injury, diagnosis, or age. Second, the leader can select members who have the same type of adaptation problem but in varying degrees. Third, the leader can select members who have a variety of adaptation problems. Regardless of the criteria of composition, the leader should compose the group so that it will be a cohesive one.

There are no methods that can guarantee a cohesive group. According to Yalom (1970), "There appears to be a general clinical sentiment that heterogeneous groups have advantages over homogeneous groups for intensive interactional group therapy" (p. 193). He goes on to say, "Although group cohesiveness is by no means synonymous with therapy outcome, there is considerable evidence . . . that cohesiveness is positively related to outcome and may be considered a way station or an intervening variable" (pp. 197–198). Functional group leaders are not required to compose heterogeneous groups, but they should attempt to create cohesive ones.

In composing a group the leader aims to select members who have similar goals, abilities, and needs and can function together in a particular action or activity. It is unlikely, therefore, that a recently admitted patient with a cerebrovascular accident would be assigned to a group with patients who are preparing for immediate discharge. The treatment goals and functional abilities would be too diverse. By contrast, two patients preparing for the homemaker role, one with an upper extremity fracture and one with joint inflammation from arthritis, might be quite compatible members of the same group. Again, the goals of the group and the treatment modality or activity process need to be considered when choosing members for a specific group.

147

Group Size

The size of a group will influence how the members relate to each other and other facets of the group experience. There is no strict rule on size. According to Yalom (1970), five to ten members is an acceptable number for an "interactional therapy group." He considers approximately seven members ideal (p. 215). We agree with this figure; seven members can work together effectively in the activity of the group and participate fully in the process of the group. Yalom (1970) also points out that if a group has fewer than five members, the opportunity for maximal member interaction decreases and the therapy becomes more leader-centered. When the group size increases beyond ten members, there is less time for individual members. In our practice we found that size should be based in part on members' attention spans, functional abilities, and ability to delay gratification. If members have problems in these areas, groups for these individuals should have fewer than five members. Again following Yalom (1970), leaders should compose a group with two more members than the ideal size. One or two members will drop out at the beginning, and the two additional members will ensure that overall size does not fall below the minimum needed. Leaders should also consider special problems related to settings. In acute care settings, patient turnover is high and rapid discharge is common. The size of the group should be large enough to absorb sudden changes in membership.

Structuring the Group and Tasks

The functional group uses occupational performance (purposeful action) to achieve treatment goals. To do this, the group should be structured to accomplish specific aspects of working in a group that will in turn lead to the ultimate goal. The group should be designed to achieve:

1. Maximal involvement of members through group-centered action
2. Maximal sense of individual and group identity
3. A "flow experience"
4. Spontaneous involvement
5. Member support and feedback

As Yalom (1983) points out, "Group leaders provide structure for the group by delineating clear spatial and temporal boundaries; by adopting a lucid, decisive, but flexible personal style; by providing an explicit orientation and preparation for the patient; and by developing a consistent, coherent group procedure" (p. 108).

Maximal Involvement

Maximal involvement is achieved through four steps. The leader must make each step clear and set the pace for the members.

Step 1: Orient the Group to the Design. The leader should first explain the nature of the group and purpose of the session(s). The leader and member roles, as well as specific goals, should be made explicity in the leader's introductory remarks to the group. The group format or structure should make sense in terms of the group members' specific needs and perceptions.

Step 2: Explain Procedures to Group. After the orientation, the leader should explain the procedure(s) to be used in the session(s). The group methodology, specific tasks, sequence of activities, agenda, and purpose must be stated in an unambiguous manner.

Step 3: Set Up the Task. Depending upon the nature of the group and the abilities of the members, the leader may involve the group in setting up the task or may do this for the group.

148

Step 4: Follow-up. After the group participates in the task, the leader assists the group in assessing the experience. The leader guides the group in connecting the task experience to the group goals and individual member goals.

Maximal Sense of Individual and Group Identity

The therapist must create a climate of safety within the group through support and genuine caring. The tasks should be structured so that members feel in control of the process. This is accomplished by involving the members in setting goals, selecting and implementing tasks, and follow-up. The therapist designs these experiences at the level of the members' abilities. An open group may require the therapist to highly structure these procedures.

149

Flow Experience

In structuring a flow experience, the leader attempts to create opportunities or challenges for action. This involves creating an environment that stimulates curiosity and the desire to achieve. Csikszentmihalyi (1975) describes a "model of the flow state," which should serve as a guideline for the therapist. He states,

> When a person believes that his action opportunities are too demanding for his capabilities, the resulting stress is experienced as anxiety; when the ratio of capabilities is higher, but the challenges are still too demanding for his skills, the experience is worry. The state of flow is felt when opportunities for action are in balance with the actor's skills; the experience is then autotelic. When skills are greater than opportunities for using them, the state of boredom results; this state again fades into anxiety when the ratio becomes too large. (p. 49)

In designing a task that will enable the members to achieve a "flow experience," the leader should include only those tasks that are culturally acceptable to the members and can of themselves produce personal satisfaction.

Spontaneous Involvement

The leader must guide the group toward discussion and action in the present; this is achieved through modeling behaviors and feedback. In addition, the activities should be structured so that action is required. The leader in turn relates the group's and individual member's behavior to the purpose of the session(s).

Support and Feedback

During a session, the leader should demonstrate specific modes of support to encourage members in their participation. The leader should follow these basic principles.

1. The leader points out universal elements, needs, concerns, and reactions to group members.
2. Members are never criticized, blamed, or made to feel isolated.
3. The activities are structured according to the range of member ability.
4. The leader is empathetic and teaches members how to give feedback constructively.

Specific skills such as empathy and genuineness, modeling behavior, giving feedback, and reality testing are discussed in detail in Chapter 5.

Conclusion

The leader role in the design stage is of critical importance to the group's ultimate success. In this stage, the leader must assess the need for a group, determine group goals and methods, develop a plan, select group members, and structure the group and its tasks. In developing a group plan, the leader aims to create a structure for facilitating purposeful, self-initiated, spontaneous, and group-centered action. Although a carefully monitored group structure has been emphasized in this chapter, one should also bear in mind that contingency or alternate plans may be called for. The initial plans are preliminary. The group format may need to be adapted when the group begins its sessions or as it proceeds through its various stages of development. To illustrate the principles and concerns of the design stage, general group plan protocols have been included for the two groups described in the case studies.

Case Study Number 1

OPEN OCCUPATIONAL THERAPY GROUP

Group History

---

1. *This group has existed on the psychiatric in-patient unit for 3 years. It is expected to continue as a part of the unit's occupational therapy program. This is an open group, with the membership changing on a weekly, sometimes daily, basis. Because the membership changes, the group is always, in a sense, in the design stage as well as proceeding through all the functional group stages. The chief of psychiatric services, a psychiatrist, has ultimate authority over the goals and structure of any therapies conducted on the unit. The occupational therapists have direct responsibility for designing, implementing, and evaluating the groups they conduct.*

2. *The occupational therapists, or for our purposes the functional group leaders, established the criteria for group membership. After assessing the needs of the hospital's psychiatric inpatient population, the leaders, in consultation with the staff, determined that at any given time there would be eight patients in need of such a group. Because the inpatient unit is an acute, voluntary, open psychiatric service, the group, herein named the Project Group, has voluntary membership.*

3. *The group meets daily for $1\frac{1}{2}$ hours. It is an open group and daily attendance is required. Usually there are new members entering and departing from the group on a weekly and sometimes daily basis.*

4. *In addition to the Project Group, patients attend daily community meetings, group psychotherapy, individual counseling, and occupational therapy sessions. Most members are also being treated with psychotropic medications or are being evaluated for such treatment. Each patient has his own case manager. All treatment is supervised by the patient's attending psychiatrist.*

5. *Some of the patients are readmissions and have attended the Project Group in prior hospitalizations. Other patients have no group treatment experience or have had psychosocial treatment in other settings.*

151

Assessment of Members

---

1. Assessment of Group Members (Including Range of Behaviors)
   A. General description
      Patients primarily live in the communities surrounding the hospital area. The group is being conducted on the psychiatric in-patient unit of an urban private general hospital. The unit has 16 beds and an interdisciplinary staff consisting of mental health counselors, nurses, occupational therapists, psychiatrists, psychologists, and social workers. Most patients are middle-class to upper middle-class blue- and white-collar workers. All hospitalization costs are being covered through third-party payers. Diagnoses include affective disorders, schizophrenic disorders, personality disorders, substance use disorders, and eating disorders. Some patients have medical problems, such as cardiac conditions, arthritis, diabetes, and multiple sclerosis, but these are stabilized and secondary to the psychiatric disorder. All patients are between 16 and 70 years of age.
   B. General description of members' expected environment
      All group members are expected to return to their homes in the community or to find a more suitable living arrangement in the community. All members are either parents, workers, students, or retired.
   C. Description of current performance in areas of occupational behavior
      Work: *Two members are college freshmen, three are homemakers, one is retired, and two are employed (accountant and freelance writer).*
      Self-care: *All are independent in basic self-care; they have difficulty making decisions when human transactions are involved in their self-care or care of their environment.*
      Leisure: *All members have expressed dissatisfaction with their use of leisure time. Some feel they have few to no interests; are all consumed with work, or do not have the resources (people, places, money, and so forth) to participate in avocational activities.*
   D. Cognitive behavior
      Members are able to understand simple written and verbal

instructions, and can concentrate on a structured task minimally for 30 minutes and maximally for 90 minutes. All have intact memory skills. Members are well-oriented to time, place, and person. The majority of members have some insight into current difficulties. Some members have difficulty sequencing a plan of action when solving problems, while others are able to make abstract judgments but have difficulty with simple decisions involved in daily living.

E. Psychosocial behavior
    Members have difficulty recognizing and verbalizing their emotions. Although members are able to imitate behaviors, they have difficulty identifying when a change in action is needed. Some members rely totally on others to fulfill their needs, while others are unwilling to accept suggestions or help. Most members are unable to identify their strengths and focus their discussions on limitations. Several members are unable to handle frustration with a task and show anxiety by not completing the activity, moving about restlessly, or being irritable while attempting to complete the task. Members attempt to interact with others in a group by always offering help (often to the exclusion of asking for help), by demanding assistance and withdrawing if it is not immediately available, or by vacillating between these extremes.

F. Physical and neuro-motor behavior
    All members are ambulatory, have adequate gross and fine coordination and range of motion to perform routine activities of daily living. They are all able to maintain balance when performing table activities, walking, and running. Many are unable to perform tasks with the strength and endurance required for the members' prehospitalization routines, for example they may take frequent rests, or complain of strain or fatigue.

G. What is the significance of these factors with regard to individual member goals and forming or planning the group or group session(s)?
    In order to promote total participation, ideally the group should be composed of no more than eight members (men and women) and have two leaders (one male and one female). The group will need to be advised on how to select

153

relatively short-term activities with little complexity and opportunity for error. The leaders will need to assume an active role in adapting the activities so that a variety of group membership roles can be practiced. They will also need to observe the group's process, suggest alternative behaviors, and assume group membership and leadership roles when the members are unable to do so. A highly supportive, genuine, and consistent emotional climate must be established and reinforced by the leaders.

2. Assessment of Group Context (The Facility)
   A. General description of program in which group is included (administrative structure)
      The group is part of the milieu therapy program offered to patients on the psychiatric inpatient unit. It is a service provided by the hospital's staff occupational therapists working on the unit. The inpatient unit is one of the services offered through the hospital's department of psychiatry.
   B. General description of physical environment
      The unit has a long hallway with eight semiprivate rooms, with a kitchen at one end, and the nurses' station, occupational therapy room, staff offices, and community living room at the other end. The occupational therapy room has one long rectangular table, a small circular table, work benches, and activity supply cabinets along the walls. The room is painted in soft beige; patients' projects are scattered about; and there are many hanging plants over a large work sink.
   C. General description of emotional climate
      The emotional climate varies according to the patient population on the unit. At times the atmosphere appears calm and quiet, and at other times it is noisy, high-keyed, and energetic.
   D. Frame of reference, purpose, and objectives
      Using a bio-psycho-social model, this short-term unit provides a safe environment for patients who have demonstrated self-destructive behaviors. Its primary purpose is alleviation of acute symptoms of the patient's psychiatric condition, evaluation, and referral to outpatient services in the community.

154

E. What is the significance of these factors for forming or planning the group or group session(s)?
    Because of the high patient turnover, the sessions will have to be held and planned on a daily basis. Closure will have to be structured with every session, as will the opportunity for discussion.

3. Assessment of Environmental Supports and Constraints
    A. Facilities and materials
        A wide range of activities can be conducted in the occupational therapy room and kitchen areas. The unit is not, however, large enough to accommodate group activities that require a lot of movement, physical sports equipment, or space.
    B. Scheduling
        Because of the other treatments scheduled, the hospital meal schedule, and patient visiting hours, the group meeting time is on a fixed schedule.
    C. Group norms and prior therapy group experience (if any)
        Physically or verbally abusive behaviors are not allowed on the unit. Patients who are unable to respect this requirement, or require a locked unit for their own safety or the safety of others, are referred to other facilities. Patients who do not participate in their treatment program, as established by the individual patients and staff, are terminated from the inpatient service. Patients who require long-term treatment on an inpatient unit are referred to other facilities. Alcohol and other nonprescribed drugs are not permitted on the unit. Smoking is only permitted in the community room (when therapy is not in session). Some members have had no prior therapy experience; others have been in groups on prior admissions or in other facilities.
    D. Do any of the environmental constraints require modification of the group, or could you alter the situation (such as locating needed materials)?
        Under the leaders' supervision, the group could use the hospital grounds and surrounding areas for activities that require a lot of space and movement, such as sports.

155

General Group Plan Protocol

A Typical Group Protocol in the Design Stage

A. Name of Group___*Project Group*___

B. Time/length of meeting(s)___*Monday-Friday, 10:30–12:00 PM*___

C. Place___*General Hospital Acute Psychiatric Inpatient Unit: Occupational Therapy Room*___

D. Open___X___or Closed Group _____
Statement of rationale:
Maximum length of stay is 6 weeks; average length of stay is 2 to 4 weeks; 16-bed unit.

E. Group Goals:
Depending on the specific group, these may include primary and secondary objectives and leader objectives for group as a whole and/or individual members.

1. Goals (*behaviors* you wish to increase or decrease)
   To be able to contribute ideas, in the group, for the selection of a group project.

   To be able to carry out selected aspects of the group project in the presence of others in the group, for example, get and distribute materials to group members.

   To be able to verbally express satisfaction about my own interaction in the group, contribution to the project, and the group's final product.

   To be able to assume group maintenance roles such as encourager, compromiser, and gatekeeper. For example, make statements such as: "Let's try it," "Can we do what some members want to do today and what the rest want to do tommorrow?," or "Let's not pick a theme until we hear every opinion in the group."

   To be able to assume group task roles, such as asking for information, giving opinions, or expressing wishes.

2. Rationale for goal selection
   On admission, members presented problems such as poor self-esteem; withdrawal from family, friends, or co-workers; loss of interest in avocational activities;

156

indecisiveness regarding what was usually "routine" decision-making; and an inability to complete tasks required for daily functioning, such as food shopping, physical care of children, and banking.

3. Outcome criteria for successful goal attainment in session(s) stated in *behavioral* terms

> *At least once in every session, each member gives or seeks information; follows through with an action step necessary for the completion of the group project; and laughs, jokes, or smiles.*

F. Group Composition or Criteria for Selecting Members

> *Ideally the group should include both men and women, and a maximum of eight members. In addition, prospective candidates for the group should minimally be able to communicate verbally in a simple manner; understand simple communications, for example, written and verbal instructions; concentrate on a structured task within the presence of seven other patients and two therapists, for a minimum of 30 minutes; and understand the goals and methods of the Project Group.*

> *It is expected that members will have a variety of occupational behavior problems. Usually prospective group members have psychiatric conditions that influence their abilities to fulfill social needs; feel masterful or useful; and meet obligations of social roles such as parent, worker, community member, or player.*

G. Leadership Roles and Functions

> *The Project Group has two leaders. Their primary roles and functions are to establish a group structure that encourages a high degree of membership involvement in the group's task and selected processes; protect the safety of individual group members and the morale of the group as a whole; encourage action within the range of member abilities and perceptions of such; act as resource persons for the making of projects and elements of group process and dynamics; and communicate knowledge of members' adaptive behaviors and maladaptive behaviors to the group and unit staff.*

H. Characteristics of Group Contract

> *Members are expected to attend sessions on a regular basis unless unusual circumstances prevail and the leaders*

are notified prior to the session in question. The members are also required to remain in each group session for 1½ hours or to negotiate with the group or leaders if a special contract or arrangement is necessary because of extenuating circumstances.

Material discussed by other group members is not to be shared outside of the psychiatric unit patients and staff. Physical and verbal abuse is not tolerated in the group. If members are unable to fulfill the requirements of the group contract they will be terminated from the group.

I. Group Methods and Procedures to be Employed:

Briefly describe or list methods, techniques and modalities.

Graded structured activity
Group process and task analysis
Group process and task adaptation
Crafts, horticulture, expressive art, and cooking

Case Study Number 2
CLOSED OCCUPATIONAL THERAPY GROUP

Group History

1. This group format has been offered at the occupational therapy clinic for the past year. The group consists of eight consecutive sessions over a 2-week period. The chief occupational therapist and chief physiatrist have ultimate authority over the group's goals and structure.

2. The group is voluntary and composed of a maximum of eight members. The members are patients at the Rehabilitation Hospital, are 17 years of age or older, both male and female, and are to be discharged within 2 to 3 weeks. Patients referred to the group are those needing help with energy conservation, time management, and adjustment to a disability. The group is thus named the Energy Conservation/Time Management Group.

The occupational therapist screens patients upon physician or occupational therapist referral. Patients must be oriented, able to communicate verbally and understand oral instructions, relatively emotionally stable, and able to concentrate on a task for 60 minutes.

The group was started because patients seen in the out-patient clinic expressed a need for more input and support during discharge. They found the return home very stressful and complained of strained family and co-worker relationships, fatigue, depression, anxiety, and feeling useless. In fact, the first of these groups was started as a peer support group—with the consultation of an occupational therapist. It later became institutionalized as part of the clinic program when the staff found that patients in the support group required less follow-up care.

3. *This is a closed group with required attendance. The group meets four times a week for 2 weeks.*

4. *The structure of the group includes eight units. These segments are sequenced to parallel and facilitate a group's phases of development. The group is intended to teach skills and at the same time develop into a group-centered, cohesive support group. The group leaders, the occupational therapists, have the power to change the group's structure as long as the goals remain the same in regards to discharge planning.*

5. *The group is developed along the model of a functional group.*

Assessment of Members

1. Assessment of Group Members (Including Range of Behaviors)
   A. General description
      Seven adults ranging from 31 to 66 years of age. There are four females (two are post-cerebrovascular accident, one has arthritis, one has multiple sclerosis) and three males (one has alcoholism, one is post-myocardial infarction, one has chronic undifferentiated pain). All are mildly de-

pressed or anxious. All members live in suburban areas and cities within a 2-hour drive of the hospital.

B. General description of members' expected environment
All members will return to live at home alone, with spouses, family members, or children. Two members are retired, two are homemakers, one is unemployed, one runs a small family business, and one is a teacher.

C. Description of current performance in areas of occupational behavior
Work: *The range of member work skills includes full to partial homemaking skills, full employment potential to being unemployed with work potential (e.g., functions at task independently for 60 minutes, held maintenance job for three years), and being retired and completely dependent on family with no interest in work.*
Self-care: *The range of member self-care skills includes complete independence in physical daily living skills (i.e., grooming and hygiene, feeding/eating, dressing, functional mobility, functional communication, object manipulation) to partial dependence in small object manipulation, wheelchair mobility, transfers, functional ambulation, grooming/hygiene, and eating.*
Leisure: *The range of member leisure skills includes recognition of avocational interests to no ability to identify activities or social situations that are perceived as playful or fun. All members express concern regarding their ability to adapt leisure activities, schedule, or home environment to enable participation in avocational pursuits. Many members have difficulty identifying community resources available for leisure activities.*

D. Cognitive behavior
All members are able to concentrate on a task or concept for 60 minutes, are oriented to person, place, and time, and have immediate and recent memory. Range of insight varies from excellent to poor. Problem-solving ability ranges from able to make decisions to total reliance on concrete cues for evaluating decisions and plans.

E. Psychosocial behavior
Most members seldom initiate conversation with individuals other than the staff or their own family members; all

express concern and anxiety over their appearance and ability to be productive or loved.

F. Physical and neuro-motor behavior

Many members become restless and agitated when expected to perform an activity. Several members have various degrees of physical dysfunction from a stroke, arthritic condition, neuro-muscular disorder, chronic pain, general lethargy, or disuse of body. The range of problems includes poor dexterity and incoordination in fine motor tasks or gait, limited active range of motion, fatigue or strain when using muscular force required for certain activities, poor sensory awareness and postural balance, and poor visual-spatial awareness.

161

G. What is the significance of these factors with regard to individual member goals and forming or planning the group or group session(s)?

In order to promote total participation, ideally the group should be composed of no more than eight members (men and women) and have two leaders (one male and one female). The group will need to be advised on how to select relatively short-term activities with little complexity and opportunity for error. The leaders will need to assume an active role in adapting the activities so that a variety of group membership roles can be practiced. They will also need to observe the group's process, suggest alternative behaviors, and assume group membership and leadership roles when the members are unable to do so. A highly supportive, genuine, and consistent emotional climate must be established and reinforced by the leaders.

2. Assessment of Group Context (The Facility)

A. General description of program in which group is included (administrative structure)

The group is one of the treatment services offered through the occupational therapy department to inpatients of the hospital. The leadership responsibility rotates among the occupational therapy staff of 18 certified therapists. Supervision is provided by the director of occupational therapy. Consultation services are also available from the staff physicians.

B. General description of physical environment

Large occupational therapy clinic with adapted kitchen, prevocational area, activity area with tables and chairs, and reception desk and offices in foyer of clinic space. The clinic is wheelchair accessible.

C. General description of emotional climate
Cheerful, warm, friendly, relaxed, and supportive. Therapists are open and direct with patients.

D. Frame of reference, purpose, and objectives
Bio-psycho-social/ecological; rehabilitation and prevention services in a private rehabilitation hospital.

E. What is the significance of these factors in forming or planning the group or group session(s)?
Because the clinic space is used by other therapists treating patients in one-to-one therapies, a room divider will be required, as will coordination of use of supplies and equipment with other staff therapists.

3. Assessment of Environment Supports and Constraints

A. Facilities and materials
All materials are within easy access. Audio-visual equipment will be borrowed from the hospital supply area.

B. Scheduling
The group is scheduled in the morning, during the busiest portion of patients' treatment schedules, so the leaders will need to make arrangements with head nurses who coordinate patient rehabilitation programs. Some patients will need transportation aides to bring them to and from the occupational therapy clinic.

C. Group norms and prior therapy group experience (if any)
None.

D. Do any of the environmental constraints require modification of the group or could you alter the situation (such as locating needed materials)?
The group time might be rescheduled to 4:00–5:00 PM, when the occupational therapy clinic is least crowded and patients have more flexibility in their schedules.

General Group Plan Protocol

A Typical Group Protocol in the Design Stage

A. Name of Group___*Energy Conservation/Time Management Group*___

B. Time/length of meeting(s)___*9:00–10:00 AM; eight consecutive sessions in 2 weeks*___

C. Place___*Rehabilitation Hospital, In-patient Services, Occupational Therapy Clinic*___

D. Open_____ or Closed Group___X___

Statement of rationale:
This group is focused on issues related to discharge planning. It is therefore limited to patients who will be discharged in 2 to 3 weeks.

E. Group Goals:

Depending on the specific group, these may include primary and secondary objectives, leader objectives for group as a whole and/or individual members.

1. Goals (*behaviors* you wish to increase or decrease)
Leader objectives:

Evaluate performance problems related to occupational behaviors necessary for functioning in life roles.
Discharge planning:

Patient referral for out-patient/home treatment services
Member objectives:

To identify changes in living environment and relationships necessary for adaptation to current disability. This includes the need for orthotics, prosthetics, and assistive/adaptive equipment, as well as the maintenance of such equipment and involvement of other individuals such as family members.

To identify potential barriers to adjustment to community living; for example, overindulgence of family members, architectural barriers, physical isolation, limited mobility, or emotional withdrawal of friends, family, lover, and co-workers.

To identify role changes necessary as a result of disability; for example, homemaker roles, work roles, or avocational roles.

To describe programs for intervening with potential barriers; for example, to be able to ask for help and receive help; to plan alternate routes and modifications of physical environment so that mobility is increased; to be able to give and receive feedback; to suggest compromises or alternatives.

To be able to prevent or minimize debilitation through organizing activities and schedule to minimize energy output.

To use joint protection and/or body mechanics principles to minimize stress on joints.

To be able to physically position self so that optimal functioning in life roles is feasible.

To be able to select, perform, and coordinate activity schedule in order to maintain a balance between rest, sleep, work, and leisure needs and interests.

To identify a peer support network in the community to aid adjustment to disability.

To describe abilities and strengths.

2. Rationale for goal selection

    These goals were selected because the members' discharge environment involves dealing with changes in life roles such as asking other people to fulfill some needs (e.g., personal care or care of usual responsibilities). It is also recognized that although members are expected to be functioning at maximum potential at discharge, they need strategies and support to physically, emotionally, and socially maintain themselves in the community. Similarly, patient education is necessary to prevent further debilitation or disability. Currently, patients have been observed to be highly dependent on staff to fulfill needs and interact on a parallel level with other patients in the hospital. Families of the patients have expressed concern over being able to cope with a disabled person at home.

3. Outcome criteria for successful goal attainment in session(s) stated in *behavioral* terms

    Changes are made in member's home environment to ac-

commodate or prevent further disability; for example, changes in furniture heights, family member available to transport patient to work, etc.

Members seek and offer assistance in group; share concerns in group; seek and offer suggestions in group.

Members conduct a meeting or phone friends, employer, or family while in hospital to discuss changes necessary to resuming or modifying role activities.

Members plan out a weekly schedule for post-discharge week, incorporating units of work, rest, play, and sleep equivalent to energy output level of predischarge week.

In doing group activities, members position themselves and protect their joints so that they can complete projects with minimal stress and at a maximal level of functioning.

Members have the phone numbers of at least two individuals they can call for support when discharged from the hospital.

F. Group Composition or Criteria for Selecting Members

The group is composed of a maximum of eight men and women patients who are 17 years of age or older. Usual diagnoses include neurological disorders (e.g., stroke, multiple sclerosis, Guillain-Barré syndrome), arthritis, cardiac disease, alcoholism, and chronic pain. Patients must be 2 to 3 weeks predischarge. They also should be oriented and able to concentrate on a task for 60 minutes, able to communicate verbally and understand oral instructions, and relatively emotionally stable (i.e., not emotionally labile or a potential suicide risk).

G. Leadership Roles and Functions

Two leaders will conduct this group. The sessions are planned into eight units, designed and implemented by the group leaders. One leader will have responsibility for screening patient referrals and introductory interviews. The other leader will have responsibility for writing notes in the patients records and for making discharge plans. The responsibilities for these functions will rotate between the leaders after completion of an eight-unit group.

H. Characteristics of Group Contract

Members are required to attend all eight sessions. They must express an interest in sharing their concerns about discharge with other group members and be willing to participate in the group's activities. They must have prior permission and a referral from their attending physician.

I. Group Methods and Procedures to be Employed
    Briefly describe or list methods, techniques, and modalities.

Session #1 Introduction to the group: a discussion of its purpose, goals, and procedures.
           Icebreaker exercise.

Session #2 Individual collages: group picks theme; group discussion.

Session #3 The "Pie of My Life" pre- and posthospitalization: an expressive art activity.
           Discussion.

Session #4 Energy conservation: lecture, slide show, demonstration, practice, and discussion.

Session #5 Time management principles: lecture, problem-solving exercises, and discussion.

Session #6 Community resources: information and referrals. Dealing with human and architectural barriers: discussion, role play, follow-up discussion.

Session #7 Activities configuration.
           Discussion.

Session #8 Establish resource network.
           Discuss termination, group review, and evaluation.
           Party.

Note. These plans would be modified according to the group's needs. For example, if the group has members of a predominant age, sex, functional impairment, or with common roles, the sessions would focus on issues related to these concerns.

References

Barris, R., Kielhofner, G., and Watts, J. H. (1983). Psychosocial Occupational Therapy: Practice in a Pluralistic Arena. Laurel, MD: Ramsco.

Csikszentmihalyi, M. (1975). Beyond Boredom and Anxiety: The Experience of Play in Work and Games. San Francisco: Jossey-Bass.

Hemphill, B. J. (ed.) (1982). The Evaluative Process in Psychiatric Occupational Therapy. Thorofare, NJ: Charles B. Slack.

Mosey, A. C. (1973). Activities Therapy. New York: Raven Press.

Yalom, I. D. (1970). The Theory and Practice of Group Psychotherapy. New York: Basic Books.

Yalom, I. D. (1983). Inpatient Group Psychotherapy. New York: Basic Books.

7

Stage 2: Formation

"Events which strengthen bonds between members enhance the potency of the group." (Yalom, 1975, p. 120)

The formation stage of a group begins at the first meeting. This event is marked by a combination of anticipation and apprehension on the part of the leader and the members. The predominant processes, during the initial sessions of the group involve orientation and exploration by all participants; as members get acquainted, learn how the group functions, and develop norms that will shape their behavior in the group. They may also explore their own hopes and fears about the group situation and try to formulate their personal goals. They may deal with issues of feeling "in" or "out" of the group, perhaps even make a decision to stay in the group and get involved, or to leave. The manner in which the leader deals with these behaviors will, to a large extent, determine the degree of trust and cohesiveness that will be present at any time during the life of the group.

171

      The specific aspects of the group that characterize the formation stage include: (1) personal feelings of belonging and acceptance, (2) dependence upon the leader and testing the leadership, (3) individual versus group goals, and (4) trust versus mistrust. These are listed here roughly in the order in which they arise in many groups, but the order may vary according to the design of the particular group. Each of these aspects will be discussed in this chapter in relation to the characteristics of the actions of the functional group (Table 7-1). These actions are (1) the purposeful (task) action, (2) the self-initiated action, (3) the spontaneous or "here-and-now" action, and (4) the group-centered action.

      The features of the initial sessions of a group that meets over a period of time may also be pertinent to the starting phases of individual group meetings. Each separate meeting is a microcosm of a series of group sessions; each meeting passes through the stages of formation, development, and termination. The starting segments of individual group sessions commonly exhibit the characteristics of the early group meetings. It is not unusual for a group to spend the final minutes of a meeting planning for the next meeting and then to spend the initial period of the subsequent meeting altering the previously made plans. Establishing control over the group's manner of functioning is one of the group-centered actions that develop during the formation stage of the group.

TABLE 7-1.
GROUP MEMBERSHIP NEEDS RELATED TO ACTION:
FORMATION STAGE

Formation Stage Issues	Purposeful Action	Self-initiated Action
Concern over belonging and acceptance	Action that includes all members 1. structured 2. successful outcome for all	Acceptance of "polite" social behavior Support for expression of negative and positive feelings
Dependence on leader Testing leader style	Strong leader involvement in task selection and adaptation Guidance regarding expectations of member roles	Leader encouragement of exploratory role Behavior-risk taking
Clarification of individual and group goals	Clear options and alternatives in goal selection An accepting climate	Expression of individual goals Behavior-risk taking
Testing for trust	Respect for opinions and feelings of members An accepting climate	Group support and encouragement for individual roles and goals Behavior-risk taking

TABLE 7-1.
Continued

Spontaneous (Here-and-Now) Action	Group-centered Action	Leader Skills Employed
Encouragement of expression of ideas, feelings and thoughts related to here-and-now action	Established pattern of interaction Beginning knowledge of group resources	Analysis and adaptation Genuineness and empathy, listening and responding
Opportunity to interact with leader and to test degree of freedom and control	Gradual sharing by members in leadership Leader input as needed Leader support	Modeling Tentativeness Feedback Sharing rationale for leader action Genuineness and empathy, listening and responding
Sharing of member perceptions and reactions as to what is going on in the group	Examination of group goals and exploration of norms appropriate to reaching group goals	Concreteness Classification Genuineness and empathy, listening, and responding
Experience support and acceptance of diversity Sharing of member perceptions and reactions to what is going on in the group	Group-centered decision-making process Developing concensus Awareness of group's own process	Climate setting for supportive interpersonal relationships. Discussing confidentiality Structuring action for member comfort and growth Genuineness and empathy, listening and responding

Group Actions

Each of the four types of action of the functional group serves to facilitate the achievement of the members' ultimate goals. Also, each involves a response to the four issues related to this stage.

Purposeful Action

The purposeful action of the formation stage in the functional group can contribute directly to the feelings of acceptance and belongingness of group development. All members need to be included and to participate in the group action. Eric Berne (1963) wrote, "The principle concern of every healthy group is to survive as long as possible, or at least until the task is done" (p. 77). For a group to work together on a task, individuals must be drawn together as members in the group, and individuals will be drawn to a group that promises to meet their needs and interests. Therefore, the purposeful action of the beginning group must be an activity that will interest, and assure the participation of, the members. Since the prospect of success also increases group attractiveness, the activity must be carefully matched with the skill level of the participants so that members can expect a successful outcome. The leader must seek opportunities to guide the action at the proper level of challenge for the group members, thereby creating a "flow experience."

Member acceptance and belongingness are also increased when the purposeful action of the formative stage provides a fair amount of structure. A clear structure helps new members recognize quickly and easily what behavior is desirable in the group, and this in turn helps them to feel more comfortable. A structured task supplies the members with clearly definded roles, goals, and limits, thus reducing member anxiety. For example, a common activity in a new group is an exercise called an icebreaker. The action goal of this exercise is to help members learn each others' names and to establish contact and communication with each other. The directions are simple and clear. All members participate, in turn, according to the structure of the particular exercise, and member interaction is achieved.

The specific purposeful action of the group influences the degree of authority the leader holds in the group. When the activity is structured, the leader holds an authoritative role; when the task is less structured, the leader holds less authority and the members hold more, leaving them to exercise more control over their actions.

The purposeful action (or task) thus regulates in part the degree of dependence or independence exhibited by members in the group. By the choice of a task, the leader can influence the extent to which members will function independently or dependently.

In a similar fashion, the purposeful action of the formative stage aids the inclusion of both group and individual goals. The character of the purposeful action provides the structure for reaching specific goals, and, through participation in selected tasks, the group establishes and clarifies its goals.

The manner of carrying out purposeful action is also closely associated with the level of trust or mistrust in the formative stage of the functional group. When the comfort level of the group is high, trust is enhanced. When the comfort level of the group is low, mistrust is common. Further, a task successfully completed enhances trust. Members usually start to give each other feedback, both positive and negative, on aspects of the purposeful action of the group. As the group begins to acknowledge this type of feedback and act upon it, group trust and cohesiveness develop. The leader can teach members how to give and receive feedback constructively through the example that he provides.

Self-initiated Action

After an initial introduction by the leader and a brief synopsis of the general goals of the group, there is usually a period of dramatic silence when members become anxious and do not know how to respond. The early sessions are characterized by the members' uncertainty over how to behave. This period of self-initiated action commonly takes the form of polite, stereotypic social behavior. For example, members will seek acceptance through polite social conversation. Members who feel awkward during moments of silence will seek to keep the conversation flowing on almost any topic. Other members who feel most comfortable with action will become impatient to get started on any kind of group task or activity and will make comments about their activity interests.

Member self-initiated action in the formation stage is usually directed toward the leader. Members in the functional group, commonly patients in treatment programs, at the outset feel highly dependent upon the leader for guidance toward personal therapeutic goals. They see the leader as a figure of authority, and the patient as a person who complies with that authority. Frequently members look to the leader to make them feel comfortable and to reduce their anxiety and discomfort. When these hopes are not realized, there may be resistance and hostility directed toward the leader. It is common for members of new groups to direct their statements to the group leader rather than to their fellow members. As time goes on, leader dependence may shift to the opposite extreme of counter-dependence. Members may display resistance to leadership, becoming highly suspicious of the leader and afraid of being manipulated. This resistance may be manifested in dissatisfaction with details about the arrangements for the group, such as the time or place of group meetings.

176

Once members are acquainted, self-initiated action takes a different form. Gradually questions about group goals emerge and members begin to discuss, clarify, and develop goals. Through taking risks and verbalizing personal fears or perceptions about what is happening in the group, members help build a climate of trust. According to Carl Rogers (1969), "If this self-initiated learning is to occur, it seems essential that the individual be in contact with, be faced by, a real problem. Success in facilitating such learning often seems directly related to this factor" (pp. 58–59).

Spontaneous Action

At first, there is little spontaneity as members seek acceptance through polite conversation about current or past events. Member listening skills are usually poor, and an exchange of ideas may be difficult. Suggestions are made, but there are few respondents to support or explore them. As time passes, positive and negative opinions are verbalized, and as these opinions are supported a climate of respect for the feelings and opinions of individual group members develops. From his extensive experience with groups, Carl Rogers (1970) states, "Curiously enough, the first expression of genuinely here and now feeling is apt to come out in negative attitudes towards other group members or towards the leader. Frequently the leader is attacked for failure to give proper guidance to the group" (p. 18). A sense of belonging in the group increases with the exchange of ideas, feelings, and reactions.

The issue of dependence on and independence from the leader is highlighted throughout the here-and-now action stage. On the basis of their group experience, members realize that the leader neither answers all their needs nor makes all decisions. As the leader refers tasks to the group, members learn to be less reliant on the leader. They begin to test the amount of freedom and control they can manage within the setting of the group. They also begin to feel more comfortable with group silences and learn to tolerate them with less anxiety.

The process of establishing norms and goals in a group helps the group interact in the "here-and-now" context because norms refer to immediate concerns. Immediacy gives impetus to a genuine exploration of conflicts and problems, as members share their own reactions to what is happening in the group. Through interaction and sharing, members deal with individual concerns about being pressured or forced by the group to conform against their will or inclination. Within this spontaneous action, group trust can grow as individual members experience support and tolerance for diversity. The development of trust in the early stages of a group, according to Corey and Corey (1982), requires a climate of respect for the opinions and feelings of group members.

177

Group-Centered Action

As the formative stage of the group progresses, group-centered action develops. As members begin to feel a sense of belonging and acceptance, a climate of respect for the individual emerges, and members become better listeners and communicators. This climate encourages members to assume more leadership roles; in some instances members may even challenge the leader. As the leader relinquishes some of his responsibility to the group members, the members and the leader develop a different relationship. Interdependence develops as the group works out new procedures, norms, and values appropriate to reaching its goals and using its resources. *Interdependence* in this context is defined as learning to accept dependence when it is truly needed and relying on leader and member expertise to help the group to function.

In their research on early group decisions, Gibb and Gibb (1967) observed that at the beginning of the formation stage, poor decision making is characteristic of group-centered action. As the emotional and social needs of the members are met, and the group develops norms of individual support, members begin to re-state and re-examine the group goals, taking the necessary time to seek every member's opinion and to establish a group consensus. These group-centered activities contribute to an atmosphere of trust, and it is not uncommon at this point to find members raising issues of confidentiality in order to test the degree of group trust.

The ultimate goal of the formation stage is to achieve a "psychological group." According to Bradford (1978), a psychological group forms under specific conditions:

1. Patterns of interaction are proven effective;
2. Differences in perceptions about task, communication, and procedures are clarified;
3. Relationships to other persons and groups are delineated;
4. Standards for participation are set;
5. Methods of work that elicit rather than inhibit member contributions are established;
6. A respected "place" for each person is secured; and
7. Trust is established among members. (p.5)

Leader Functions and Intervention Strategies

The four group actions described above are initiated and directed by the leader. In this section, we consider the role of the group leader in the formation stage and present strategies for effective leader participation. Two primary issues of the formation stage are members' need for acceptance and the development of relationships with the group leader. The group leader can facilitate these processes through specific strategies.

Setting the Climate

As the organizer of the group, the leader sets the climate. The term *group climate* refers to the ongoing attitudes and concepts that pervade the group. Apart from specific strategies, the leader's interpersonal style will, to some extent, influence the group climate. The warmth and acceptance of the leader and the ability to convey respect for each member contribute to a supportive group climate. In their report of research studies of therapy groups, Truax and Mitchell (1971) wrote that a supportive and empathetic relationship with the leader is positively correlated with member progress in treatment. They also report that there is a significant positive correlation between the degree of support offered by the leader and group member outcome; that is, the more support offered by the leader, the better the results achieved by the members.

During the early group sessions, as members search for a type of behavior that is acceptable in the group, they are dependent upon the leader for guidance. Both openly through their statements and covertly through their actions, they look to the leader for direction and structure as well as approval. The leader may well wonder how much structure should be provided at this point. Yalom (1983) favors a middle ground between too much structure and too little structure. He writes, "Although patients desire and require considerable structuring by the therapist, excessive structure may retard their therapeutic growth. If the leader does everything for patients, they will do little for themselves. Thus, in the early stages of therapy, structure provides reassurance to the frightened and confused patient; but persistent and rigid structure, over the long run, can infantalize the patient and delay assumption of autonomy" (p. 123). It seems that while members like the leader who provides the greatest structure, they are less likely to achieve therapeutic changes when working with such a leader.

One of the roles of the leader is to teach members to assume responsibility for themselves and their group. This can be accomplished by sharing the rationale for leader actions with the members. By modeling certain behaviors, the leader can also teach members to increase their participation through a variety of roles. This method of teaching was presented in some detail in Chapter 5. The leader of the functional group can reduce the importance of the leader role by assuming the role of a consultant or trouble shooter.

The leader can support the members in a variety of ways. According to Yalom (1983), "The therapist supports by treating the patient with respect and dignity. The therapist supports by identifying and reinforcing the patient's strengths and virtues. The therapist supports by refraining from undermining defenses but instead by bolstering them and by encouraging patients to employ defenses that are at least one step more effective than the one they are currently using" (p. 128).

The leader should create a climate that is experienced as constructive and supportive, one in which members feel safe and can learn to trust the group. Genuine trust takes time and hard work. Members cannot trust each other unless they know each other, respect one another, and believe that they will be listened to and that a sincere attempt will be made to understand them. Trust grows from working and learning together. A group may be successful, but still not achieve trust among its members.

Clarifying Goals and Norms

The group leader should state the purposes and goals of the group at the first session. Leaders may also wish to express personal feelings, hopes, and expectations that they have for the group. For instance, the leader of a group may begin with the following statement. "In this group we are going to work hard and at the same time have some fun together. We will meet every Wednesday from 10:00 AM to noon in this room and I expect you to attend all meetings. From time to time there will be new members joining the group. We are going to learn to plan group meetings together and then to complete the tasks that we have planned. This group is meeting to help you with your social relationships so that you can learn to interact more appropriately in your work situation or with your family. I am looking forward to being part of this group, to getting to know you, and to working with you to achieve our goals." The leader may then pause and invite member reactions and comments. While the goals as stated may be clear to the leader, they may not be clear to the members. Members should be encouraged to ask questions and make comments.

Through this introductory statement, the leader has established specific norms for group behavior. First, the group can talk about its goals, task, and the perceptions of its members. Second, the leader will participate in this process. Third, the responsibility for planning and learning will be a total group responsibility. Fourth, regular group attendance will be expected, and this is an open group where new members may be expected. Finally, it is all right for members to have fun in the group.

If the leader continues to model the established norms as the group progresses it will help the group create a safe climate for learning that will form the basis for group effectiveness. Napier and Gershenfeld (1983) present a list of norms that the leader can encourage. They are adapted here for the leader of the functional group.

1. People should be listened to and recognized. The leader should acknowledge a questioning look or tentative statement. The norm of personal respect and equal rights of membership in the group is established.
2. The group is a safe place. Members are reassured that what happens in the group stays within the group. A member will not be ridiculed or reprimanded for speaking out. The lead-

er's behavior can be discussed just like any other point of discussion in the group. The leader will encourage quiet members to speak more often and talkative members to speak less often.

3. Feelings are important. The leader encourages the expression of feelings and establishes the norm that the expression of feelings is vital if the group is to use its energy toward resolving problems and reaching its goals.

4. Objectivity is encouraged. The group learns that when the leader asks for information from members, or asks if others have similar feelings to those expressed, those feelings are not dismissed or smoothed over as nonexistent. The leader encourages observers and observation in order to demonstrate that all members can look at what is happening in the group.

5. Members learn from doing things and analyzing them. In the process of achieving the goals of the group, focusing on "here and now" is a major learning method.

6. Planning is a joint effort. The leader is involved with the members in planning for group sessions. The leader does not have sole responsibility for the success of the group.

These norms, established through the leader's actions, provide examples that influence the behavior of the members and invite members to participate in various group roles.

Clarifying goals, both group goals and individual goals, is crucial in the early stages of the group. Further, this is an ongoing process throughout the life of the group, not something that is done only once at the outset. As the group gains experience, members become better able to formulate goals. Through their involvement helping others to identify ways of learning from the group, members get a better idea of how they too can profit from the group experience, and they thus become more adept at stating personal goals. At this point, the leader may be able to help members to develop contracts with the group as a method of reaching their personal goals. A contract is a statement made by the member to the group regarding what he or she is willing to do during a group session, or even outside of the group meeting. This contract states specific behaviors the member is willing to explore or change. Through the contract, the member assumes responsibility for his or her behavior and takes an active role in personal behavioral change.

Selecting Purposeful Action

A primary purpose of the formation stage is to assist members to feel accepted and included as valued members of the group; therefore, a purposeful action needs to be carefully selected and adapted by the leader. In discussing the planninng stage of the group (Chapter 6), the leader was advised to evaluate the level of member skills. It is particularly important in the early session of the group that the leader select group tasks in which all members are assured of experiencing success. Again, the tasks should also be appealing to all group members. Finally, the purposeful action of the group sessions should be selected for its ability to draw in all members, both on the real and the symbolic level.

The leader must decide how much control to exercise over the group. Will the leader or the members be in control? The relative importance of control will vary according to the characteristics of the members. Control is a major problem for some individuals, and tasks must be chosen by the leader with this problem in mind. For instance, if a group of adolescents has trouble accepting adult leadership, the leader should select a task with limits and controls that are inherent in that particular task. Through varied task selection and adaptation, the group leader can adjust the amount of control needed by the group to enable it to reach treatment goals.

Conclusion

Analysis of the types of behavior that may appear in this stage should indicate that the leader has a variety of techniques and strategies available to guide the group members as they begin their work as a group, but also that the leader cannot completely control the group behavior. Leaders must expect and prepare for certain standard behavior patterns adopted by individuals confronted with an entirely new set of circumstances. Careful planning in the use of resources will enable the leader to build a cohesive and functioning group.

In the following pages, we continue with our case studies by including complete protocols for sessions and evaluations for the open and closed groups in the formation stage. These case studies provide the reader with concrete examples of functional group work.

Case Study Number 1
OPEN OCCUPATIONAL THERAPY GROUP

"Breaking the Ice": A Typical Group Session in the Formation Stage

---
Group Session Plan Protocol

A. Name of Group_____*Project Group*_____
   Date__*June 6*_____

B. Specific goals for the group session
   Given a leader-structured and directed task members are:
   To learn other group members' names;
   To talk to another group member and the group as a whole.
   To take turns talking in a group.

C. Specific goals for group members if different from above, and goals for each group member
   Gary, Eric, Liz, and Pearl: To express their feelings and re-actions to being members of a group with four incoming new members.
   New group members: To decrease feelings of anxiety about being in the group and increase feelings of acceptance and belonging.

D. Description of and rationale for methods and procedures
   Explain group goals, leader and member roles, group structure and limits (to help members understand the purpose of the group's activities and to instill feelings of safety and belonging).
   Describe icebreaker activity in simple and clear fashion (to decrease tension in group and help members feel less isolated).

E. Description of and rationale for leadership role
   The leaders should optimally provide enough task structure and support so that members feel reassured that they are safe, yet not be too rigid or directive as to encourage overly dependent behavior on the part of group members.

F. Describe necessary preparations
   Review session plan among co-leaders.
   Gather supplies necessary for group activity.

Prepare new members for group in individual pregroup interviews.

G. List material and equipment needed
Eight pieces of 8½ × 11″ lined writing paper
Eight sharpened pencils with erasers
Pencil sharpener

H. Time and sequence outline for sessions, including what you will do and say as leader, and what the group will do; consider both content and process.

Explain group's purpose, leader and member roles and expectations (approximately 5 minutes).

Explain that because there are so many new members in the group today, the leaders have planned an activity in order to help group members get to know one another. Pass out a piece of paper and pencil to each group member. Ask that everyone write down their first and last name on the top of the paper. Then explain that each person will first write down two things they like about their name, and two things they might not like about their name. After completing this part of the activity, the leader explains, each member will share what they have written down on the paper with the person sitting to the right of them. Once everyone has completed this part of the activity, it is further explained, then members will take turns introducing their partner by sharing what that person said they did and did not like about their name. The group is told that upon completing this activity members will be encouraged to talk about their reactions to this activity (approximately 10 minutes).

Group will then do the described activities. The leaders will encourage member participation, keep group activity within time limits of session by prompting group to complete various aspects of task, and clarify directions as needed (approximately 60 minutes).

Leaders will summarize group's purpose and discuss potential plans for the following session with group members (approximately 15 minutes).

I. Other information pertinent to this specific session:
For example—will there be any new members, co-leaders, or guests; is there an unusual tone on the unit or special

event that is about to occur or just occurred for the individual member or group?

In this session, half of the group will be composed of new members.

Session Evaluation Form Protocol

A. Name of Group_____*Project Group*_____
   Date_____*June 6*_____

B. Were the goals accomplished? (Give rationale and state outcome.)
   Partially. Gary had difficulty taking turns speaking in group and interrupted several times while other group members were talking. Bette, a new group member, remained in the group for 10 minutes and left saying she was too "nervous" to sit any longer. All other members accomplished the session goals.
   Was the session helpful in accomplishing short and long term group and individual member goals?
   Yes, except for Bette (see above).
   Do you have any evidence that the session(s) have been helpful to the members' functioning (adaptation) outside of the group?
   Yes. The leaders have observed group members informally chatting on the unit at lunch.

C. Was the group structure adequate for accomplishing the goals? Give rationale and consider: leadership; time/length of meeting; open vs. closed group; time, sequence, methods and procedures; media/modalities/techniques employed; norms/behaviors reinforced implicitly or explicitly; methods of reinforcement; and stage of group's development.
   Partially. For most of the group members, the structure established a nonthreatening climate.
   Did the structure provide optimal "action" or "flow activity" for a "flow state" to occur?
   Yes. For the most part, members interacted in a spontaneous manner when paired with another member. However, the leaders

should take on more directive roles during future group discussions.

Did the structure provide optimal purposeful, self-initiated, spontaneous, and group-centered "action" for cognitive and emotional impact, skill learning, and adaptation to occur through "occupation"?

Given the group's stage of development, the structure did encourage members to interact in an optimal fashion. Hence, with leader input, the members completed the structured group task.

Did the structure provide for new learning, reinforce ment of current level of functioning, or adaptation, or did it reinforce functioning below current level of adaptation? Explain and give rationale.

The structure encouraged all members to learn the value of sharing concerns in a group. Except for Bette, the range of group processes enabled members to participate at a parallel through cooperative level.

Did the structure provide an opportunity for evaluation and feedback regarding the group procedures and member progress? Explain.

Yes. Members were encouraged to discuss their reactions to the session and ideas for future sessions. The leaders had ample opportunity to observe member behavior/reactions to varying degrees of task structure.

D. What changes would you make in group goals and structure for the next session, or if you were to lead this session again?

In the event that there are an uneven number of members remaining in a group, I would avoid group activities requiring dyads.

E. Were you adequately prepared for the session? (Give rationale, considering such things as time, place, materials, and physical and emotional environment.)

Yes. Knowing there would be four new members was essential to the preparations, including planning a structured exercise.

F. How did you function as leader? How did your behavior and role affect the group? Were you effective? (Give rationale.) What did you learn about yourself as group leader?

When Gary had difficulty taking turns and Bette said she was leaving the group, I had to assume the group maintenance roles. Members responded by imitation and began to encourage each other to listen and share. I believe this was effective because it helped to model group norms and encouraged group-centered participation.

G. Was the group interaction as you anticipated? If problems occurred, what processes can you identify as a basis for understanding the problems?
I did not anticipate that Bette would have difficulty remaining in the group. The expectation that she remain in the group for 90 minutes appeared to overwhelm her.

H. In the future, what might you do differently as group leader? (Give rationale.)
I would speak with the nursing staff prior to the session to establish if any special events occurred prior to the session. Based on this information, I might make alternate agreements ("contracts") with patients who "need" to grade the amount of time spent in the group. For example, Bette could have been told she could stay in the group for 15 minutes the first time, 30 minutes the second, etc., thereby encouraging success and establishing helpful limits.

187

Case Study Number 2
CLOSED OCCUPATIONAL THERAPY GROUP

A Problematic Group Session in the Formation Stage

Group Session Plan Protocol

A. Name of Group _____ *Energy Conservation/Time Management Group*
   Date _____ *second session out of eight—December 15*

B. Specific goals for the group session
   To learn value of peer support and group problem solving.

C. Specific goals for group members if different from above, and goals for each group member
Leader goal: to encourage group cohesiveness.
D. Description of and rationale for methods and procedures
Group discussion
Expressive art activity
Rationale: to increase trust, member sharing, and goal setting by establishing an environment that fosters free expression of common concerns.
E. Description of and rationale for leadership role
Encourage expression of fears and perceptions in here and now
Clarify group goals and task
Rationale: to enable group to establish a balance of group and individual goals and assure that the group is a safe place to express concerns.
F. Describe necessary preparations.
Gather art materials.
G. List material and equipment needed.
Magazines, glue, scissors, large construction paper, tape, and a variety of precut magazine pictures
H. Time and sequence outline for session including what you will do and say as leader and what the group will do; consider both content and process.

1. *Introduce group to activity: state purpose, goals, and methods (approximately 5 minutes).*
2. *Encourage group members to pick a group theme for the individual collages they will make. Explain the theme might be about, for example, discharge from the hospital. Assume group maintenance and task roles as needed by group (approximately 10 minutes).*
3. *Members make collages with leader assistance/adaptation as necessary. Members are encouraged to help each other and ask for help when needed (approximately 30 minutes).*
4. *Encourage members to share perceptions regarding the group theme and its relationship to their collages and the group's goals.*

I. Other information pertinent to this specific session: for example—will there be any new members, co-leaders, or

guests; is there an unusual tone on the unit or special event that is about to occur or just occurred for the individual member or group?
None.

Session Evaluation Form Protocol

A. Name of Group___*Energy Conservation/Time Management Group*___

Date___*December 15*___

189

B. Were the goals accomplished? (Give rationale and state outcome.)

Partially. Members expressed their individual fears about discharge; however, only one or two members saw the value of the group for support or relevance of group goals.

Was the session helpful in accomplishing short- and long-term group and individual member goals?

Yes. In order for members to establish trust and a feeling of belonging to the group, it is necessary that a balance between individual member and group goals be negotiated and tested in the group.

Do you have any evidence that the session(s) have been helpful to the members' functioning (adaptation) outside of the group?

No.

C. Was the group structure adequate for accomplishing the goals? Give rationale and consider leadership; time/length of meeting; open vs. closed group; time, sequence, methods and procedures; media/modalities/techniques employed; norms/behaviors reinforced implicitly or explicitly; methods of reinforcement; and stage of group's development.

The value of the group activity was not easily apparent to members. A more structured goal setting activity is preferable for this stage of the group's development.

Did the structure provide optimal "action" or "flow activity" for a "flow state" to occur?

No. Members needed more time to talk about their individual concerns.

Did the structure provide optimal purposeful, self-initiated, spontaneous, and group-centered "action" for cognitive and emotional impact, skill learning, and adaptation to occur through "occupation"?

No. As typical of the formation stage, members had difficulty assuming responsibility for the group and for making group decisions.

Did the structure provide for new learning, reinforcement of current level of functioning or adaptation, or did it reinforce functioning below current level of adaptation? Explain and give rationale.

Members were able to verbalize their individual concerns regarding managing life tasks upon discharge. By being encouraged to share these concerns, members began to talk about what they wanted rather than what their family and friends wanted.

Did the structure provide an opportunity for evaluation and feedback regarding the group procedures and member progress? Explain.

Yes. Members were actively encouraged to give the leaders feedback.

D. What changes would you make regarding group goals and structure for the next session, or if you were to lead this session again?

   Use a more individual-centered activity, with the specific aim of goal setting.

E. Were you adequately prepared for the session? (Give rationale, considering such things as time, place, materials, and physical and emotional environment.)

   I was not prepared for the degree to which members wanted to talk about their fears.

F. How did you function as leader? How did your behavior and role affect the group? Were you effective? (Give rationale.) What did you learn about yourself as group leader?

   I learned that although the value of the group is apparent to me, members need time to learn the value it has for them. Hence, a group decision-making task was too premature for this stage of the group.

G. Was the group interaction as you anticipated? If problems occurred, what processes can you identify as a basis for understanding the problems?

I expected more group problem solving and group-centered support than was realistic. Member trust and more group experience are necessary to achieve those ends.

H. In the future, what might you do differently as group leader? (Give rationale.)

I would assume a more active role in structuring an individual task for group members and assume more of the group maintenance roles.

191

References

Berne, E. (1963). *The Structure and Dynamics of Organizations and Groups.* New York: Grove Press.

Bradford, L. P. (1978). Group Formation and Development. In L. P. Bradford (ed.), *Group Development.* La Jolla, CA: University Associates.

Corey, G., and Corey, M. S. (1982). *Groups: Process and practice* (2nd ed.). Monterey, CA: Brooks/Cole.

Gibb, J., and Gibb, L. (1967). Humanistic elements in group growth. In J. Bugenthal (ed.), *Challenges of Humanistic Psychology.* New York: McGraw-Hill.

Napier, R. K., and Gershenfeld, M. K. (1983). *Making Groups Work: A Guide for Group Leaders.* Boston: Houghton Mifflin.

Rogers, C. (1969). *Freedom to Learn.* Columbus, OH: Merrill.

Rogers, C. (1970). *Carl Rogers on Encounter Groups.* New York: Harper & Row.

Truax, C., and Mitchell, K. (1971). Research on certain therapist intrapersonal skills in relation to process and outcome. In A. Bergin and S. Garfield (eds.), *Handbook of Psychotherapy and Behavior Change.* New York: John Wiley & Sons.

Yalom, I. D. (1975). *The Theory and Practice of Group Psychotherapy* (2nd ed.). New York: Basic Books.

Yalom, I. D. (1983). *Inpatient Group Psychotherapy.* New York: Basic Books.

8

Stage 3: Development

Individuals are unique, therefore one can rightfully expect that patterns in the development of a group will vary from group to group. Nevertheless, all groups demonstrate certain features. We have explored this principle in our examination of the aspects common to the formation stage. In this chapter we describe the features characteristic of the group's development stage. More specifically, this chapter emphasizes leadership issues and individual and group expectations. The topics of assessing progress and identifying and managing problems are discussed in the context of the group's *action* in the development stage. The leader's functions and intervention strategies in the development stage are explained. These functions include involving members in setting goals, adapting the task to the stage of the group and individual members, and encouraging group member roles. Again, we apply these concepts to the two case studies.

195

Issues and Expectations

The life of a group is multidimensional. At a concrete level, the functional group is composed of individuals, an activity, and a physical environment. At a symbolic level, the group has a purpose, both implicit and explicit; a set of dynamics and processes; and internal and external motivational forces. All these factors are interacting at any given moment. In a sense these factors define the group's "meta-space" which is not something one can stop in time. The meta-space is an experience of the moment. Neutral observers and group members could probably describe the group in similar ways, yet, it is likely each would also experience it a bit differently. Hence, the concrete and symbolic levels of a group are not readily distinguishable.

The purpose of the group is the health and adaptation for its members. To accomplish this purpose the leader strives to create an environment conducive to purposeful, self-initiated, spontaneous, and group-centered action. Since groups progress through stages with unique characteristics (Cohen and Smith, 1976; Corey and Corey, 1982; Garland and Frey, 1970; Garland, Jones, and Kolodny, 1973; Klein, 1972), the leader must use a variety of strategies. Thus, the leadership functions in the development stage may vary a great deal. Our intent, therefore, is to suggest a general scheme for assessing the group's ongoing progress and identifying and managing problems. Certain issues are typical of this stage, and each can be met with appropriate responses (see Table 8-1).

TABLE 8-1.
GROUP MEMBERSHIP NEEDS RELATED
TO ACTION: DEVELOPMENT STAGE

Development Stage Issues*	Purposeful Action	Self-initiated Action
Concern over acceptance or rejection as result of change Testing the safety of the group	Goals and structure Minimal risk in task Clear and consistent rules, limits, expectations, and routines Protection from attack	Encouragement and support for exploratory behavior
Struggle between safety and involvement	Clear options and alternatives	Encouragement for task involvement and expression of positive and negative reactions and feelings
Control and power struggles (conflict) with leader and other members	Consistency and safety of individuals Support and encouragement for member leadership Task appears useful to each individual	Permissive environment Opportunity for action matches individual member abilities

*Corey, G., and Corey, M. S. Groups: Process and Practice (2nd ed.), p. 194. Copyright ©
1977, 1982 by Wadsworth, Inc. Reprinted by permission of Brooks/Cole Publishing Co.,
Monterey, CA.

TABLE 8-1.
Continued

Spontaneous (Here-and-Now) Action	Group-centered Action	Leader Skills Employed
Encouragement and support for initiative taken in group and expression of thoughts and feelings in here-and-now As action occurs, group-centered leadership encouragement Modeling of group task and maintenance roles	Explicit group norms Recognition and clarification of stage issue in context of dependence vs. independence theme Clarification of reality	Genuineness and empathy Listening and responding Concreteness Reality testing Group task analysis and adaptation
	Encouragement for cohesive member sharing of task roles Leader input as needed by group Recognition and clarification of stage issue in context of intimacy theme concerning passivity vs. activity or personal vs. group wishes and needs	Modeling behavior Self-disclosure Feedback
	Flexibility in assuming leadership and social-emotional roles as able Support and encouragement for member leadership Recognition and clarification of stage issue in context of dependency vs. counterdependency needs or ambivalence regarding autonomy theme	Confrontation

Assessing Progress

In order to assess the group's progress, we suggest that the leader and whenever possible the group attempt to identify problems at the concrete and symbolic levels. Such a review might occur at the beginning of a meeting, at the end of a session, at the completion of a task, or intermittently during the session. Some therapists prefer to designate a period of time for evaluating the session, such as the last ten minutes. Other leaders might feel that this sort of strict scheduling breaks the flow of action or activity. We suggest that issues or problems be addressed as they occur in the group. The timing will depend ultimately on the individual leader's style and on the group members' attention span, ability to delay gratification, and the immediacy of the problem. Regardless of these considerations, in every instance it is essential that the leader evaluate the group and individual members' progress.

Structured and unstructured observation methods are used to assess the group's ongoing progress. Structured methods provide the leader and members specific formats for systematically noting and recording behavior, events, and reactions. In addition to the methods suggested in Chapter 5 (see Figs. 5-2, 5-3, 5-4, 5-5 and 5-6), the members or the leader may choose to design observation formats specifically suited to the group's needs. In contrast, unstructured observation methods require the leader or members to examine progress by spontaneously analyzing the group's process and dynamics. Miles (1981) suggests two techniques for the study of group behavior particularly relevant to the functional group in the development stage: "trainer process comments" (p. 115) and "intermittent process analysis" (p.117). "Trainer [or leader] comments (a) illuminate the immediate problems facing the group, and (b) help build in the process-analysis function as a central feature of the group's work structure" (p.115). Miles suggests that once the group has some experience with trainer process comments, the group can establish that members should spontaneously comment on what is happening in the group. "In effect, group members are continually asking, 'What is happening? What is making these things happen? How can we change our behavior for the better?'" (p. 117).

If the members are encouraged to be evaluators and observers in order to determine the validity of leader assessment, the methods should yield data pertaining to the group's outcomes and operation at the symbolic and concrete levels. The information gathered concerns members' actual functioning in the group environment and reports of behavior outside the group. Two questions guide the assessment. First, as a result of the group's interaction, are members learning the skills and occupational behaviors necessary for adaptation, and are they better able to fulfill their health needs? Second, is the group's structure, process, and content conducive to appropriate action in the development stage? (See Table 8-1.)

Identifying and Managing Problems

In the development stage one may expect problems that are characteristic of groups learning to work on a mutual task. Problems may derive from the group as a whole or from individual members. In attempting to identify the group's needs, the leader must ask a basic question. What is inhibiting the group's movement toward purposeful, self-initiated, spontaneous, group-centered action? The leader must examine every aspect of the functional group in order to answer this question.

Bradford, Stock, and Horwitz (1978) mention some of the more common group problems. These include "conflict or fight," "apathy and nonparticipation," and "inadequate decision making" (p. 63). They also suggest specific origins for these group problems. Members who demonstrate *fight* behavior may view the group and themselves in one of four possible ways. They may feel *"frustrated because they feel unable to meet the demands made of them"* (p. 63). Their main goal may be *"to find status in the group"* (p. 64) rather than follow the goals or task set by the leader or other members. The members may feel a greater loyalty to *"outside groups of conflicting interests"* (p. 64). Finally, the members may *"feel involved and are working hard on a problem"* (p. 64) and therefore resent the disruption or conflict from others. Members may respond with *apathy* if *"the problem upon which the group is working does not seem important to the members, or . . . [seems] less important than some other problem on which they would prefer to be working. . . . [Or] the problem may seem important to members, but there are reasons which lead them to avoid attempting to solve the problem"* (p. 67). Members also respond with apathy when a group has *"inadequate procedures for solving the problem"* (p. 68). Related to this is the feeling that members are *"powerless about influencing final decisions"* (p. 68). Finally, *"A prolonged and deep fight among a few members . . . [may have] dominated the group"* (p. 68), leaving others to feel apathetic.

Inadequate decision-making may result from unsatisfactory group interactions. For example, "there has been premature calling for a decision, or the decision is too difficult, or the group is low in cohesiveness and lacks faith in itself. . . . [Or again] the decision area may be threatening to the group, either because of unclear consequences, fear of reaction of other groups, or fear of failure for the individuals" (p. 72).

In addition to the group's difficulties with task and maintenance functions, individual members may have problems. A group member may lack the skills or experience necessary to accomplish his role or function in the group. A group member may also have unrealistic notions regarding his skills or ability to complete the task. In discussing action, Csikszentmihalyi (1975) points out that "perhaps the most salient element of the flow state is a sense of control over the environment. A person has to feel that his ability to act is adequate to meet the opportunities for action available. 'Inner' skills and 'outer' challenges must be in balance before the flow state can be experienced" (p. 191).

The problems of individual members vary, and the leader should consider the following problem areas when trying to identify specific problems:

1. Lack of opportunity for skill practice and modeling
2. Inadequate positive reinforcement
3. Secret or conflicting goals
4. Inadequate information
5. Ill-formed defense mechanisms
6. Poor self-esteem
7. Lack of task skills or social interaction skills
8. Physical, neuro-motor, or cognitive limits to functioning
9. Overappraisal or underappraisal of skills
10. Overappraisal or underappraisal of environmental demands

Problems can also arise on the symbolic level; problems in the group's structure and processes can inhibit a group's development. Although we assume that group leaders have positive intentions, they may lack group leadership skills or be unaware of the ways in which they are fostering group problems. Some of the problems often stemming from group leadership are:

1. Failure to match the activity to the group's abilities, processes, goals, or environment.

2. Failure to meet members' interests or basic needs (safety, approval, self-esteem).
3. Group goals are unclear, unrealistic, or not understood.
4. Emotional environment does not support the group's efforts or those of individual members.
5. Group members lack the necessary skills to perform a specific task.
6. The leader is unaware of secret or conflicting goals because mechanisms for receiving feedback are not established or the information is not heard.
7. The physical climate is not conducive to achieving the group's purpose. (The room is too hot or too small; the group is too big for everyone to be heard or understood.)
8. The composition of the group does not allow for cohesiveness.
9. Members are not encouraged to contribute to the goals of the group, to the group procedures, or to help each other directly.
10. The leader does not encourage the group to evaluate its procedures, process, and effectiveness.
11. The distribution of leadership and membership roles is inadequate.
12. Group members are not given the opportunity to test ideas and possible courses of action.
13. The leader does not establish clear limits and expectations, or is passive in dealing with disruptive group behavior or interference from outside the group.
14. The leader shows favoritism to particular group members or to subgroups through nonverbal or verbal communication.

If a leader is concerned with his or her leadership style, this list can serve as a guide for self-examination, supervision, and identifying leadership problems. In some instances, solving an apparently minor problem of the physical environment can eliminate apparent leadership problems. For example, if members feel they are not heard adequately, a change from a noisy room may create an environment in which leader and members are more relaxed and therefore can listen to each other more easily. An advantage of coleadership is that leaders can share the task of identifying problems. One might more naturally follow and address leadership problems at the concrete level of the group, and the other attend to problems at the symbolic level.

Leader Intervention Strategies

Many strategies can be used to intervene in the numerous problems just described. To influence the group's process and outcome, the leader can consciously alter the group's structure through three strategies. These are (1) involving members in setting goals, (2) adapting the task more closely to the group and individual members, and (3) encouraging group member roles. To use these methods, the leader should be familiar with the functional skills and strategies described in Chapter 5.

Involving Members in Setting Goals

An essential feature of occupational therapy is the patient's participation in his plan of treatment. As Yerxa (1967) candidly points out:

> Occupational therapy has been unique, historically, because of the client's participation in his own treatment. Choice has been so fundamental to our thinking that we have questioned whether procedures which are done *to* the person, over which he has no control, should be called occupational therapy. (p. 3)

A key leadership function in the group, therefore, is to enable the group members to become involved in establishing goals. The strategy employed varies according to the individual's readiness as well as the group's maturity or degree of social-emotional cohesiveness.

The value of member involvement in goal setting should not be underestimated. In their study of making choices, Henry, Nelson, and Duncombe (1984) found that "subjects who were not permitted choices in completing the activity perceived themselves as less powerful only when they participated in the activity in the presence of others in the same situation" (p. 249). By encouraging the group members to make choices about the group's goals, the leader establishes a norm that supports the notion that the group will reinforce members' sense of control and mastery. Rather than creating a group culture or set of norms that instill a feeling of hopelessness,

202

the leader aims to empower members by teaching, through experience or action, the value of achieving a personally selected goal. It appears likely, in light of the Henry, Nelson, and Duncombe study, that having a sense of choice is particularly important to individuals when an activity is conducted in a group setting.

Even if group goals are explicitly stated by the leader, they often appear ambiguous to the members in the initial phase of a group's development. In the case of a short-term group, with a limited time frame, the leader must rapidly focus members' attention and energy on goal setting. The many factors that influence the selection of goals by the group and individual members, as well as the recurring nature of goal selection during the group's course, makes member involvement in goal setting an ongoing leadership task.

In order to understand the intervention strategy for involving members in goal selection, we should examine factors that can influence the formation of group goals. Cartwright and Zander (1968) have identified three factors that appear to influence "goal formation." They include:

1. *Motives of members:* These can be of a personal interest to individual members or solely in the best interests of the group.
2. *Superordinate group goals:* These focus on long-term purposes and group objectives.
3. *The group and its social surroundings:* This includes other groups that exert influence on the group's goals.

Research has also demonstrated that members will take greater risks and be more willing to work together towards the group's purpose if they are involved in making a group decision or specifying a group goal (Cartwright and Zander, 1968).

How can the leader facilitate member involvement in goal setting? If the functional group is conducted within an institution or with some outside directives, the leader should first and always keep the members informed of the group's general purpose and resources. After giving general information on these factors, the leader should ask members what their needs are. Leaders can also give member feedback and encourage the members to give each other feedback about the occupational behaviors displayed in the group and their adaptiveness. Members often find it useful to hear about the procedures and formats used in similar groups. Through these various strategies the leader helps members and the group as a whole define its problems and needs.

Functional group members are often severely impaired in their ability to cognitively, emotionally, or socially impart information or formulate goals. Insecurity about performance skills, such as management of new prosthetic devices, can also contribute to difficulty in goal setting. Therefore, the leader, in the course of the group's development, must at times actively establish formats for goal setting. This can be accomplished by structuring various activities to help members clarify their goals, actively listening to members and reflecting back what is being said or not said in concrete terms, observing members and reporting back what is being done or not done, and encouraging group members to report back to the group their experiences outside the group as pertinent to the here-and-now action in the group.

Finally, it is crucial that through their verbal and non-verbal behavior leaders demonstrate that every member's opinion is important to the group's functioning. Similarly, the leader must be aware of members' changing needs and the necessity for involving members in goal setting throughout the course of the group's development.

Task Adaptation

The development stage builds on the formation stage of the group. In the first stage a group climate is established, group goals and roles are clarified, and the basis for trusting relationships is formed. As the group continues to develop, the leader must adapt the task and his or her strategies to meet the newly evolved needs of the group. The development stage includes what Corey and Corey (1982) call the *"transition stage"* and *"working stage"* of a group. They point out that "the transitional phase of a group's development is marked by feelings of anxiety and defenses in the form of various resistances" (p.194). In the functional group, certain member behaviors or "resistances" might appear: concern over group acceptance or rejection if members change, testing the safety of the group, a struggle between safety and involvement, and control and power struggles or conflicts with the leader or with the other group members (p. 194). Once the group has worked out these issues, it has passed into the working stage of a group. Members are able to function as a cohesive unit; there is open communication; the leadership functions are shared; and members feel there is hope for change (pp. 195–196). Interestingly, it is common for beginning group leaders to feel that they have done something wrong when developmental problems arise in a group. It is our belief that these problems are characteristic of groups learning to act together on a task, and that in order for the group to progress it must work through the issues specific to the development stage.

A group leader can use specific strategies in adapting the group's task structure and process in the development stage. First, the leader should identify the dominant characteristic displayed by group members. Second, the leader then grades or structures the activity to allow the group to learn how to work out the issue. For example, a leader might notice that members are late for a group meeting and do not bring the supplies necessary to complete a planned activity. By confronting the group with empathy, the leader can begin to clarify if a power struggle exists. Perhaps the leader learns that members felt the activity choice was imposed upon them by the leader or by a subgroup of members. If this is the case, the group can be supportively encouraged to examine alternative ways to approach the decision-making process. The leader might suggest that the group role play confronting an authority figure or practice ways to offer an opinion or give information. Ultimately, the leader is permitting a safe rebellion and teaching new behavior or adaptive skills by being accepting yet protecting the safety of the group.

If the group is an open group, one can expect that issues will recur as the membership of the group changes. Similarly, if the membership is heavily weighted with individuals who are experiencing difficulty with a particular problem, such as separation problems of adolescence, then one should expect that problem to be reflected in the type of group development issue that arises (*e.g.*, power and control struggle relative to the leadership or task). In a closed group, the leader has an advantage in being able to process the group's actions and plan strategies on a session to session basis. Finally, given the nature of a short-term, open group, of which there are many in acute care settings, the functional group leader must view the group's development and plan for it as it might all exist in one session. Thus one session might include formation, development, and termination stage issues. For example, the tone on a psychiatric inpatient unit might be rapidly assessed prior to the group meeting and an activity suggested to the group based on the formulation. The therapist working in an acute care setting will need to be more prescriptive or restrictive in adapting activities than would the leader working in a long-term setting.

Encouraging Group Member Roles

In order for group members to be encouraged to assume the various group membership and leaderhsip roles, they must be involved in planning the group and in assuming responsibility for action in accordance with the group's stage of development. First, members must be taught the skills necessary to engage in a group task. Such skills as giving feedback, receiving feedback, reality testing, speaking in the present tense, decision making, and assessing progress, can be modeled by the group leader or leaders and practiced by the members.

Once the group members have the prerequisite skills, the leader can encourage members to assume the task and maintenance functions of the group through the following techniques.

1. Involve all group members in defining the group's purpose, procedures, and norms, and in the observation of the group's behavior.
2. Positively reinforce members' strengths, compensate for deficits through structuring the group's task at a level members can manage, and avoid focusing on members' limitations.
3. Provide the group with the resources necessary for task completion, that is, an appropriate room and access to needed materials as shown in Figure 8-1.
4. Act as a resource person and facilitator rather than an authority or rescuer.
5. Use a co-leader, if possible, to model ways to share responsibility and to give support. In other words, do not look to the group for emotional support or supervision. Members should feel that the leader or leaders are present to enable the group to achieve positive action rather than to meet the leader's needs.

FIG. 8-1. *The working stage of a group. (Courtesy of the Towne House Creative Living Center, Oakland, CA)*

6. Provide some structure but do not overwhelm the group so that members feel useless or not understood. Too much structure fosters dependency and stifles self-initiated action.
7. Sanction testing a variety of behaviors within the limit of the group's safety.
8. Help members to assess realistically the consequences of their actions and the relationship between behavior in the group and behavior outside the group.

Conclusion

Like the formation stage, the development stage has particular issues and problems requiring specific responses by leaders. The issues that arise are part of the growth critical to the well-being of the group and its ultimate success as a group with certain goals. In the following pages, the various features and concerns of the development stage are illustrated in the group session plans and session evaluation forms completed for both groups in the case studies.

Case Study Number 1
OPEN OCCUPATIONAL THERAPY GROUP

Integrating the New Member in the Development Stage

Group Session Plan Protocol

A. Name of Group___*Project Group*___
   Date___*June 13*___
B. Specific goals for the group session
   To experience success in an interdependent task.
   To express feelings and thoughts in the present tense.
   To express positive and negative reactions and feelings.
C. Specific goals for group members if different from above, and goals for each group member
   Mary (new member): Integrate into group.
   Other group members: Express negative and positive feelings about having a new group member.
D. Description of and rationale for methods and procedures
   Summarize previous session (to reinforce learning for "old" members and to integrate new member).
   Decide on theme and group procedures for painting group mural (to provide an opportunity for expressing and processing threatening feelings regarding having a new member in the group; activity is familiar to old members and provides a role for all members; there is no one correct way to paint a mural, hence, no opportunity for failure).
E. Description of and rationale for leadership role
   Encourage members to talk about their fears and anger regarding perceived potential loss of attention in group and own anxieties when entering a new group.
   Rationale: Provides group an opportunity to reality test expectations of leader and group; recognizes stage issue of dependence vs. independence and at the same time reinforces that

it is safe to express feelings in the group; frees the group's energy for spontaneous, purposeful, group-centered action; and clarifies how individual and group dynamics can affect decision making and action.

F. Describe necessary preparations

Review and discuss plan among group leaders.

Prepare new member for group in a pregroup interview: Discuss recent activities of group, its goals and norms. Reinforce notion that new members are encouraged to participate at their own pace and that it is likely that she will feel somewhat confused, perhaps like an outsider, until she has some experience with the group's procedures and processes.

Cut paper and gather necessary supplies.

G. List material and equipment needed

Poster paints in the primary colors

Ten wide paint brushes

Paper cups, water, and tape

Large roll of paper for mural

H. Time and sequence outline for session, including what you will say and do as the leader and what the group will do; consider both content and process.

Introduction of new and old members; review of group's purpose and procedures (approximately 10 minutes).

Review previous group session with group input (approximately 5 minutes).

Plan group mural, encouraging group member roles (approximately 15 minutes).

Members paint mural (approximately 30 minutes).

Process session and plan next session—see leadership role (approximately 30 minutes).

I. Other information pertinent to this specific session:

For example—will there be any new members, co-leaders, or guests; is there an unusual tone on the unit or special event that is about to occur or just occurred for the individual member or group?

There is a new female member joining the group.

This session will take place on a Friday and the group will not meet again until Monday.

A highly esteemed group member was discharged yesterday.

Session Evaluation Form Protocol

A. Name of Group___*Project Group*___
   Date___*June 13*___

B. Were the goals accomplished? (Give rationale and state outcome.)
   Yes. All group members participated in the painting of a mural. The theme selected was "Birth and Death." Members shared positive feelings and negative reactions about the group with the new member.
   Was the session helpful in accomplishing short- and long-term group and individual member goals?
   Yes.
   Do you have any evidence that the session(s) have been helpful to the members' functioning (adaptation) outside of the group?
   Partially. In the community meeting following this group session, some members discussed the need for a unit orientation brochure.

C. Was the group structure adequate for accomplishing the goals? Give rationale and consider: leadership; time/length of meeting; open vs. closed group; time, sequence, methods and procedures; media/modalities/techniques employed; norms/behaviors reinforced implicitly or explicitly; methods of reinforcement; and stage of group's development.
   Yes. However, in the next session, it seems advisable to let the group members take a more active role in assuming the task roles.
   Did the structure provide optimal "action" or "flow activity" for a "flow state" to occur?
   Yes. By having the group members select a mural theme, they were challenged to express their feelings in an activity that matched their capabilities.
   Did the structure provide optimal purposeful, self-initiated, spontaneous, and group-centered "action" for cognitive and emotional impact, skill learning, and adaptation to occur through "occupation"?
   Yes. However, in the next session the group members should be encouraged to select an activity modality so that they can

examine their decision making process and tendency to rely on the group leaders.

Did the structure provide for new learning, reinforcement of current level of functioning or adaptation, or did it reinforce functioning below current level of adaptation? Explain and give rationale.

The structure did provide for new learning. Members learned that rather than heightening a sense of deprivation and isolation, expressing their thoughts and emotions enabled them to feel closer to other members and gratified by the group's efforts.

Did the structure provide an opportunity for evaluation and feedback regarding the group procedures and member progress? Explain.

Yes. Having a structured process time at the beginning and end of the session eased the new member's transition into the group and gave the old members the feeling they were all heard.

D. What changes would you make regarding group goals and structure for the next session, or if you were to lead this session again?

In the next session the leaders should gently encourage members to assume more of the group task roles. In adapting the leader roles members should be urged to make simple task decisions, then sequence a plan of action, and, finally, detect when a change in action is needed.

E. Were you adequately prepared for the session? (Give rationale, considering such things as time, place, materials, and physical and emotional environment.)

Yes. The meeting started on time, all the necessary materials were available, and the leaders provided a supportive, enthusiastic, and consistent environment.

F. How did you function as leader? How did your behavior and role affect the group? Were you effective? (Give rationale.) What did you learn about yourself as group leader?

I established the group's procedures for the session; encouraged members to participate in the task by asking for their opinions and feelings; and reality tested by exploring the relationship between member thoughts and feelings and behavior. I believe this was effective in bringing about a feeling of cohesiveness and safety in the group. Members became aware of similarities in their reactions. This should aid the members in assuming more responsibility for task roles and in testing out new role behaviors. I learned that it is more comfortable for me to explore member reactions when the group is involved in an expressive vs. a constructive activity.

G. Was the group interaction as you anticipated? If problems occurred, what processes can you identify as a basis for understanding the problems?

As I anticipated, members relied heavily on the leaders for task structure and emotional support. Expressing negative and positive feelings is quite difficult for members, especially with a new member present. Given these issues, members' needs for leader approval and fear of loss of attention may have fostered the dependency.

H. In the future, what might you do differently as group leader? (Give rationale.)

In the future, to reinforce the idea of member choice and responsibility, I would suggest three alternative expressive art activities.

Case Study Number 2

CLOSED OCCUPATIONAL THERAPY GROUP

Power and Control Relative to Leader and Task in the Development Stage

Group Session Plan Protocol

A. Name of Group___*Energy Conservation/Time Management Group*___

Date___*fourth session out of eight—December 17*___

B. Specific goals for the group session

To learn energy-saving procedures, work simplification techniques, and organization of the environment to minimize energy output.

C. Specific goals for group members if different from above, and goals for each group member
Recognize ambivalence over dependency on leader, hospital, and significant others.

D. Description of and rationale for methods and procedures
Lecture, slide show, demonstration, practice, and discussion
Rationale: Audio-visuals will make procedures more concrete; discussion gives members an opportunity to vent feelings and get group support; and practice allows for some skill development.

E. Description of and rationale for leadership role
Teacher, encourager, supporter, and confronter
Rationale: To model techniques, reality test, and support members' emotional needs.

F. Describe necessary preparations
Prepare audio-visuals, lecture, and work simulations.

G. List material and equipment needed
Slides, screen, slide projector, and work simulation stations

H. Time and sequence outline for session including what you will say and do as leader and what the group will do; consider both content and process.
Slide show and lecture
Group discussion
Practice techniques at work simulation stations

I. Other information pertinent to this specific session:
For example—will there be any new members, co-leaders, or guests; is there an unusual tone on the unit or special event that is about to occur or just occurred for the individual member or group?
Patients are preparing for hospital Christmas festivities.

Session Evaluation Form Protocol

A. Name of Group___*Energy Conservation/Time Management Group*___

Date___*December 17*___

B. Were the goals accomplished? (Give rationale and state outcome.)

Yes. Members were able to express concerns about being dependent on their families and their anger towards the therapist for not continuing the group post-hospitalization. Members were able to demonstrate some procedures and techniques.

Was the session helpful in accomplishing short- and long-term group and individual member goals?

Yes.

Do you have any evidence that the session(s) have been helpful to the members' functioning (adaptation) outside of the group?

Yes. Some members have requested the therapist give them written instructions to take home.

C. Was the group structure adequate for accomplishing the goals? Give rationale and consider: leadership; time/length of meeting; open vs. closed group; time, sequence, methods and procedures; media/modalities/techniques employed; norms/behaviors reinforced implicitly or explicitly; methods of reinforcement; and stage of group's development.

Session should be expanded or group held more often. The pace seemed too quick and rushed.

Did the structure provide optimal "action" or "flow activity" for a "flow state" to occur?

No. More opportunity was needed for problem solving and practice.

Did the structure provide optimal purposeful, self-initiated, spontaneous, and group-centered "action" for cognitive and emotional impact, skill learning, and adaptation to occur through "occupation"?

No. More group problem solving and open-ended simulated problem situations would have been helpful for behavioral rehearsal.

Did the structure provide for new learning, reinforcement of current level of functioning or adaptation, or did it reinforce functioning below current level of adaptation? Explain and give rationale.

Yes. All members attempted to practice the techniques and discuss how the procedures would work or be problematic at home.

Did the structure provide an opportunity for evaluation and feedback regarding the group procedures and member progress? Explain.

Yes. The group discussion gave members an opportunity to give feedback and practice exercises and gave the leaders a chance to observe.

D. What changes would you make regarding group goals and structure for the next session, or if you were to lead this session again?

I would provide members with written materials illustrating and summarizing the techniques learned.

E. Were you adequately prepared for the session? (Give rationale, considering such things as time, place, materials, and physical and emotional environment.)

No. The goals were unrealistic and materials were needed.

215

F. How did you function as leader? How did your behavior and role affect the group? Were you effective? (Give rationale.) What did you learn about yourself as group leader?

Yes, I was effective in providing support through structure and room for group support to surface by pointing out common themes, issues, and alternative behaviors.

G. Was the group interaction as you anticipated? If problems occurred, what processes can you identify as a basis for understanding the problems?

The group members were somewhat more angry than I expected. This may be due to the upcoming holidays and related feelings regarding loss in functioning and impending discharge.

H. In the future, what might you do differently as group leader? (Give rationale.)

Divide group into pairs for practice session to increase member sharing and decrease dependence on leaders for instruction and support.

References

Bradford, L. P., Stock, D., and Horwitz, M. (1978). How to diagnose group problems. In L. P. Bradford (ed.), Group Development (2nd ed.), pp. 62–78. La Jolla, CA: University Associates.

Cartwright, D., and Zander, A. (1968). Motivational processes in groups: Introduction. In D. Cartwright and A. Zander (eds.), Group Dynamics Research and Theory (3rd ed.), pp. 401–417. New York: Harper and Row.

Cohen, A. M., and Smith, R. D. (1976). The Critical Incident in Growth Groups: Theory and Technique. La Jolla, CA: University Associates.

Corey, G., and Corey, M. S. (1982). Groups: Process and Practice (2nd ed.). Monterey, CA: Brooks/Cole.

Csikszentmihalyi, M. (1975). Beyond Boredom and Anxiety The Experience of Play in Work and Games. San Francisco: Jossey-Bass.

Garland, J. A., and Frey, L. A. (1970). Application of stages of group development to groups in psychiatric settings. In S. Bernstein (ed.), Further Explorations in Group Work, pp. 1–28. Boston: Boston University School of Social Work.

Garland, J. A., Jones, H. E., and Kolodny, R. L. (1973). A model for stages of development in social work groups. In S. Bernstein (ed.), Explorations in Group Work: Essays in Theory and Practice, pp. 17–71. Boston: Milford House.

Henry, A. D., Nelson, D. L., and Duncombe, L. W. (1984). Choice making in group and individual activity. American Journal of Occupational Therapy 38(4): 245–251.

Klein, A. F. (1972). Effective Groupwork: An Introduction to Principle and Method. New York: Association Press.

Miles, M. B. (1981). Learning to Work in Groups: A Practical Guide for Members and Trainers (2nd ed.). New York: Teachers College Press.

Yerxa, E. J. (1967). 1966 Eleanor Clarke Slagle Lecture: Authentic occupational therapy. American Journal of Occupational Therapy 21(1): 1–9.

216

9

Stage 4: Termination

Termination of a group, as in most human relationships, and especially where the participants have gone through a lot together and have developed a sense of closeness and mutuality, is fraught with sadness. It is akin to losing someone dear and feeling grief, or to feeling that one is being abandoned. It leaves one with the dread of loneliness and of having to "go it alone." It reactivates the fear of risk and the anticipation of inadequacy and hence failure. Mingled with these anxieties, if the group has been a help, are feelings of hope, of power to succeed, and of the adventure of facing a new day. (Klein, 1972, p. 283)

Issues and Expectations
    Denial and Avoidance
    Premature Termination
    Anxiety and Fear
    Depression and Anger
    Sadness
    Raising New Issues for Discussion
Leader Functions and Intervention Strategies
    Encouraging Members to Express Concerns
    Discussing Feelings of Loss, Anger, and Sadness
    Dealing with Unfinished Business
    Review of Members' Participation in the Group
    Transfer of Learning to New Situations
    Reinforcing Confidentiality
Members' Action Responses
Conclusion

The process of termination must be viewed from two different vantage points: the termination of one member in an open group and the termination of an ongoing closed group. The issues and expectations of both cases are similar. The primary tasks of the termination stage are, first, a review of the group experience with an accompanying consolidation of what has been learned, and, second, dealing with the members' concerns and feelings about separation and loss.

The final meetings of a group are important because they give members the opportunity to clarify the meaning of their experiences in the group. This process makes members aware of what they have learned, what behaviors have changed, and what skills they may have acquired. In addition, members can decide which of these changes in behavior they can or want to bring to new situations.

In this chapter we describe the issues a leader can expect to face in the termination stage. Leader functions and intervention strategies for facilitating closure are also discussed. The needs of group members with regard to action in the termination stage will be highlighted. Finally, the principles discussed are applied to the two case studies through completed group session plans and session evaluation forms for the termination stage.

Issues and Expectations

The leader should expect certain reactions to the termination of an individual member or the group as a whole. Although we use the term termination to describe this stage, we discuss the reactions in terms of their transitional roles. Termination is a transition to another stage in the life of the individuals involved, and therefore the leader must guide the members into that new stage. Dealing with the following issues and reactions to termination will enable members to move beyond the group.

Denial and Avoidance

Group members may deny the reality of termination (Cohen and Smith, 1976; Klein, 1972) by not talking about it or by putting off confronting their feelings until the last few minutes, when it is too late to discuss them thoroughly. Groups may also deny the reality of termination by making elaborate plans for the group to meet again in a reunion. In this case the end of the group sessions is acknowledged, but the end of the group relationship is denied.

Premature Termination

Typically some members will withdraw from the group before issues of termination are discussed. Withdrawal is manifest through lack of participation (Cohen and Smith, 1976; Corey and Corey, 1982), lateness, or absenteeism.

Anxiety and Fear

It is quite common for group members to experience anxiety over the impending termination (Cohen and Smith, 1976; Corey and Corey, 1982; Klein, 1972). Fears usually concern the members' ability to transfer what they have learned in the group to outside situations. Such anxiety may manifest itself in regressed behavior, moving apart from the group to gain closure, or a return to behavior stereotypic of the formation and development stages of the group.

Depression and Anger

Feelings of anger may surface around the time of termination. At times this anger is not expressed and the grief is internalized; hence, members feel depressed and abandoned (Klein, 1972). The anger may also be directed toward the group in general for not having fulfilled the fantasies or goals of the member. Similarly, the anger may be directed toward the leader or the institution. Members may view the group experience as worthless and become irritated with one another.

Sadness

As the group members seek closure, members may experience intense feelings of sadness (Cohen and Smith, 1976; Klein, 1972). As a result, members may reduce the intensity of their involvement.

Raising New Issues for Discussion

Some members, under the pressure of termination, may bring up new issues for the group to consider when there is no longer time to discuss these issues adequately. It is important for leaders to be aware of this possibility and to acknowledge the importance of the issue. In addition, they must be realistic: they must point out the inappropriateness of dealing with new agendas at the time of closure.

Leader Functions and Intervention Strategies

The most important response of the leader to member reactions is to continue to acknowledge feelings as done throughout the group meetings.

Encouraging Members to Express Concerns

As in the early phases of the group, the leader needs to encourage expression of fears and expectations as members reach the final sessions of the group. These feelings may be as troubling to the members as were their initial feelings upon entering the group. The task of the leader is to remind the members that the cohesiveness and support they feel in the group today is the result of their participation in the group process. The leader should remind them that each member contributed to creating the group atmosphere that they now experience.

Discussing Feelings of Loss, Anger, and Sadness

If the leader avoids dealing with feelings of loss and anger at the end of the group, members probably will avoid doing so also. The leader must facilitate an open discussion of the feelings of loss that accompany the end of any meaningful experience. If they are not openly discussed, members will react with feelings of anxiety, depression, and anger.

Dealing with Unfinished Business

The leader must allot time for going over and discussing unfinished business relating to transactions between members or to the group process or goals (Corey and Corey, 1982). Members may need to bring up unresolved conflicts with other members or with the leader. It is not always possible to resolve the issues that are raised, but an exploration of their current state can be helpful before the group terminates. Member needs and resources should also be assessed so that appropriate referrals can be made when necessary.

Review of Members' Participation in the Group

Members have been giving and receiving feedback throughout the life of the group, and that has helped them to assess their impact upon the group. During the last sessions, more specific feedback may be helpful as part of a review of each member's participation. This process might be prefaced by asking members to report briefly how they saw themselves acting in the group and what the group has meant to them. This activity can be followed by feedback from the group concerning how they have perceived each member's participation in the group.

Transfer of Learning to New Situations

The termination stage can be a time for members to prepare for the new experiences that they will encounter in new situations or groups. The knowledge or skills they have gained from this group experience may help them cope with new situations. In the final sessions members are prepared to generalize their experiences and to relate them to situations outside the group. To integrate their experiences, Corey and Corey (1982) have suggested such activities as role playing and behavioral rehearsal.

Reinforcing Confidentiality

At the time of termination the leader should repeat the principle of confidentiality and remind members to respect confidences even after the group has ended.

Members' Action Responses

The issues raised in the termination stage lead to the membership needs related to action shown in Table 9-1. To support purposeful action, the leader should provide structure and encourage members to assume group maintenance roles. This is especially important

222

TABLE 9-1.
GROUP MEMBERSHIP NEEDS RELATED TO ACTION: TERMINATION STAGE

Termination Stage Issues	Purposeful Action	Self-initiated Action	Spontaneous (Here-and-Now) Action	Group-centered Action	Leader Skills Employed
Denial and avoidance Premature termination	More focus on maintenance roles and less on task	Moving apart from group	Becoming more individual-centered. Less focus on here-and-now; more review of group's history and life.	Withdrawal	Confrontation Modeling behavior Feedback
Anxiety and fear		Trust vs. mistrust Power struggles		Devalue importance of group and learnings	Genuineness and empathy Listening and responding Reality testing Self-disclosure Feedback
Depression and anger		Regressive behavior Conflicts with leader and other members		Anger towards leader Group conflicts predominate Lack of participation	
Sadness		Withdrawal from group Feedback to other members with less intensity		Silences and inactivity	
Raising new issues for discussion	More structure Closure	Regressive		Viewing work done as worthless	Reality testing Confrontation

because closure can activate withdrawal or strong emotions in people. These feelings may prompt members to return to behaviors displayed in the formation and development stages of the group. Hence the action is centered on individual member's needs rather than on the group's needs. Members' responses are less spontaneous, and group interactions focus on conflicts with the leader or with one another. Such responses require the leader to use the full range of skills described and noted in Table 9-1.

Conclusion

224

The termination of any role or relationship is difficult, and the leader must carefully guide the members in dealing with this stage. At this point members must make the final effort to absorb and consolidate their experiences in order to move forward and continue their progress. With the help of the leader, many members view this stage as a true transition from therapy to life outside the group. In the following pages, the principles are applied in the completed group session plans and the session evaluation forms for the two case studies.

Case Study Number 1
OPEN OCCUPATIONAL THERAPY GROUP

Separating from the Group in the Termination Stage

Group Session Plan Protocol

A. Name of Group___*Project Group*___
   Date___*June 19*___
B. Specific goals for the group session
   To enhance self-esteem.
   To increase interest in avocational activities.
C. Specific goals for group members if different from above, and goals for each group member

Group members: Express feelings of loss, anger, and sadness.
Terminating member: Express fears about leaving group; review
work in group; and discuss concerns about returning to job/
family.

D. Description of and rationale for methods and procedures
Encourage group to complete terrariums started in prior session.
Remind group that member is leaving today.
Encourage group members to discuss their feelings and reactions to member leaving.
Plan for following session by asking each member to share
what they have learned in group and what their future goals
are.
Rationale: Completing the group activity should enhance members' sense of efficacy and joy in avocational tasks. It gives
members a behavioral scheme for a similar activity outside of
the hospital. Members may deny or avoid intense feelings that
surface around termination. Exploring the issues will help
members externalize their feelings, get support, and see the
value of involvement in action with others. Planning for the
next session gives members remaining in the group a sense of
hope and continuity.

E. Description of and rationale for leadership role
Listen and reflect members' feelings back to group.
Check if perceptions are accurate.
Rationale: Members may conceal their feelings of anger and
sadness about a member leaving the group or of feeling hopeless
because of being left in the group.
Encourage members to review the group's progress by summarizing some of the recent events and asking the group to
add their reflections.
Rationale: This should reinforce what has been learned in
group and center the responsibility for future action and planning on the group members.
Ask members to report what the group has meant to them.
Rationale: This gives members an opportunity to transfer what
they learned in the group to outside situations and deal with
unfinished business with the departing member or group leaders.

F. Describe necessary preparations

Unlock and open doors to occupational therapy room and supply cabinet.
Review plan with co-leader.

G. List material and equipment needed
Small plants, potting soil, colored gravel, spoons, water, newspaper, and plastic cups

H. Time and sequence outline for session, including what you will say and do as leader, and what the group will do; consider both content and process.
Review of group plan for session and announcement of member's termination (approximately 5 minutes).
Completion of terrariums (approximately 55 minutes).
Discussion: Member termination, progress review, and planning (approximately 30 minutes).

I. Other information pertinent to this specific session:
For example—will there be any new members, co-leaders, guests; is there an unusual tone on the unit or special event that is about to occur or just occurred for the individual member or group?
Member who is departing from group has attended ten sessions.
Group members learned yesterday that the chief psychiatrist on the inpatient unit is leaving to assume a position in another hospital.
New psychiatry residents are expected to arrive on July 1, along with other student interns in psychology and social work. An occupational therapy student is observing the group today. The members do not know her.

226

Session Evaluation Form Protocol

A. Name of Group____*Project Group*____
Date____*June 19*____

B. Were the goals accomplished? (Give rationale and state outcome.)
Partially. Members expressed their anger about being in the hospital and fears regarding going home. They reluctantly completed their projects and disparagingly commented on their self-worth and the value of avocations.

Was the session helpful in accomplishing short- and long-term group and individual member goals?

Yes, in regard to long-term group goals: members recognized and supported each other's feelings. No, in regard to improved self-esteem and avocational role interest.

Do you have any evidence that the session(s) have been helpful to the members' functioning (adaptation) outside of the group?

Yes, members asked for evening passes to go to the movies.

C. Was the group structure adequate for accomplishing the goals? Give rationale and consider: leadership; time/length of meeting; open vs. closed group; time, sequence, methods, and procedures; media/modalities/techniques employed; norms/behaviors reinforced implicitly or explicitly; methods of reinforcement; and stage of group's development.

Given the many staff changes and member termination, it would have been preferable to have a group discussion prior to the task component of the session.

Did the structure provide optimal "action" or "flow activity" for a "flow state" to occur?

No. Members were feeling abandoned and self-doubting. By first completing the terrarium project, members' here-and-now reactions were diverted from reality testing and getting group support.

Did the structure provide optimal purposeful, self-initiated, spontaneous, and group-centered "action" for cognitive and emotional impact, skill learning, and adaptation to occur through "occupation"?

Yes. The opportunity to discuss feelings, summarize events, and plan for the future enabled the group to free themselves for other activities later in the day.

Did the structure provide for new learning, reinforcement of current level of functioning or adaptation, or did it reinforce functioning below current level of adaptation? Explain and give rationale.

The structure provided members an opportunity to learn how feelings can get in the way of action if they are used to reinforce a sense of passivity and helplessness rather than to assert oneself by communicating needs.

Did the structure provide an opportunity for evaluation and

feedback regarding the group procedures and member progress? Explain.

Yes. The group discussion at the end of the session encouraged members to give each other feedback.

D. What changes would you make regarding group goals and structure for the next session, or if you were to lead this session again?

I would allow silence to persist and be examined before intervening by prompting the group to complete the activity task.

E. Were you adequately prepared for the session? (Give rationale, considering such things as time, place, materials, and physical and emotional environment.)

The physical environment was adequate; however, the emotional climate was not. The group members were on the verge of discussion rather than proceeding with the task. The session was too highly structured for the emotional content that came forth.

F. How did you function as leader? How did your behavior and role affect the group? Were you effective? (Give rationale.) What did you learn about yourself as group leader?

I believe that if the emotional content were dealt with first, the group would have had more of a sense of success with their products. I learned that "listening" to the group is particularly essential in the first minutes of a session and that the session should then be adapted accordingly. By not listening, I implicitly gave the message that feelings were not important.

G. Was the group interaction as you anticipated? If problems occurred, what processes can you identify as a basis for understanding the problems?

I did not anticipate how angry and abandoned the members felt. Two members exploded at the student observer and said she was not welcome. The many changes on the unit seem to have decreased the feeling of safety in the group and precipitated a regression to issues regarding trust vs. mistrust.

H. In the future, what might you do differently as group leader? (Give rationale.)

I would actively listen to the members before encouraging them to complete the task. This would create more open communication and, hopefully, a match between member needs and the task.

Case Study Number 2
CLOSED OCCUPATIONAL THERAPY GROUP

Revival of Formation Stage Issues in the Termination Stage

Group Session Plan Protocol

A. Name of Group_____*Energy Conservation/Time Management Group*
   Date_____*eighth session out of eight—December 20*

B. Specific goals for the group session
   To establish a resource network among group members.
   To evaluate the group.
   To express feelings regarding discharge and group's termination.

C. Specific goals for group members if different from above, and goals for each group member
   To symbolize group's gains and termination by having a party.

D. Description of and rationale for methods and procedures
   Share home phone numbers.
   Review various community resources.
   Have members bake cookies and prepare fruit salad.
   Rationale: To reinforce gains and ability to be independent; to provide concrete resources.

E. Description of and rationale for leadership role
   Listen and convey empathy.
   Reality test; clarify feelings.
   Rationale: To bring closure to group in a supportive manner.

F. Describe necessary preparations
   Buy ingredients for cookies and salad.
   Schedule use of kitchen.

G. List material and equipment needed
   Flour, sugar, eggs, butter, chocolate chips, bowls, adaptive utensils, fruit, napkins, and plates

H. Time and sequence outline for session including what you will say and do as leader, and what the group will do; consider both content and process.
   Prepare food.
   Discussion (farewell and resources).
   Eat food and clean up.

I. Other information pertinent to this specific session:
For example—will there be any new members, co-leaders, or guests; is there an unusual tone on the unit or special event that is about to occur or just occurred for the individual member or group?
None.

Session Evaluation Form Protocol

A. Name of Group___*Energy Conservation/Time Management Group*___
Date___*December 20*___

B. Were the goals accomplished? (Give rationale and state outcome.)
Yes. Members prepared food for party. Expressed their sadness and joys of accomplishments in group; thoughts about returning to community and resources they might use.
Was the session helpful in accomplishing short- and long-term group and individual member goals?
Yes, for the most part. However, two members were somewhat silent and withdrawn from group.
Do you have any evidence that the session(s) have been helpful to the members' functioning (adaptation) outside of the group?
Yes. Families have reported interest in meeting other members of group when patient returns home.

C. Was the group structure adequate for accomplishing the goals? Give rationale and consider: leadership; time/length of meeting; open vs. closed group; time, sequence, methods, and procedures; media/modalities/techniques employed; norms/behaviors reinforced implicitly or explicitly; methods of reinforcement; and stage of group's development.
Yes, except for two withdrawn members. These members needed more active encouragement to share their feelings.
Did the structure provide optimal "action" or "flow activity" for a "flow state" to occur?
Yes. Members laughed and cried spontaneously. They also tolerated moments of silence together.

Did the structure provide optimal purposeful, self-initiated, spontaneous, and group-centered "action" for cognitive and emotional impact, skill learning, and adaptation to occur through "occupation"?
Yes. The cooking/baking allowed members to successfully practice what they learned and in a culturally appropriate way share their feelings about the group's termination.

Did the structure provide for new learning, reinforcement of current level of functioning or adaptation, or did it reinforce functioning below current level of adaptation? Explain and give rationale.
For the most part, members learned that they can get more support by sharing and initiating action. They were required to complete an activity using newly acquired task and social-emotional skills.

Did the structure provide an opportunity for evaluation and feedback regarding the group procedures and member progress? Explain.
Yes. The session was planned to focus on termination and evaluation, so members were prepared to evaluate.

D. What changes would you make regarding group goals and structure for the next session, or if you were to lead this session again?
I would have a written evaluation form so that the less verbal members would have an easier time giving feedback.

E. Were you adequately prepared for the session? (Give rationale, considering such things as time, place, materials, and physical and emotional environment.)
For the most part, yes (see comment under "D").

F. How did you function as leader? How did your behavior and role affect the group? Were you effective? (Give rationale.) What did you learn about yourself as group leader?
By being supportive, task-oriented, and empathetic, members were able to accomplish a task and most shared their concerns and sorrow.

G. Was the group interaction as you anticipated? If problems occurred, what processes can you identify as a basis for understanding the problems?
I did not anticipate the withdrawal of two members. The discussion of closure appeared to revive feelings of distrust and

231

anxiety present in these two members in the first few group sessions. .

H. In the future, what might you do differently as group leader? (Give rationale.)
I would take a more active role in involving the silent members and discuss the goals of each session earlier in the group. Perhaps a posted schedule of the group's goals, unit activities, and session goals would be useful to members.

References

232

Cohen, A. M., and Smith, R. D. (1976). The Critical Incident in Growth Groups: Theory and Technique. La Jolla, CA: University Associates.

Corey, G., and Corey, M. S. (1982). Groups: Process and Practice (2nd ed.). Monterey, CA: Brooks/Cole.

Klein, A. F. (1972). Effective Groupwork: An Introduction to Principle and Method. New York: Association Press.

PART THREE

Teaching and Research

In the first section of this book, we present descriptive historical and research data on groups in general and on occupational therapy groups in particular. We then outline a new model for group treatment called the functional group model. The second section of this book is devoted to the application of the functional model to therapy groups and addresses in particular the role of the group leader. In this third section, we consider the professional areas that our model for practice relies upon for acknowledgment and validation—education and research.

The functional group is the first model for group treatment to be developed in the field of occupational therapy. The model is based on the evidence of current research in the field of group treatment and group dynamics and in occupational therapy. Continuing research and evaluation will undoubtedly bring forth new evidence on the effectiveness of various techniques, and this evidence in turn will lead to modification of the concepts and principles that guide group work. The practice of group work in occupational therapy will continue to be defined and recognized through the education of therapists and the collection of research data. Anyone who develops competence in a particular field recognizes that competence must be polished, advanced, and improved. To master a particular model and its application is only the beginning of a longer journey toward its full use in helping individuals achieve their goals and meet their needs. As part of this process, the therapist will undoubtedly look to the research literature and to educational resources.

10

Concluding Remarks: Teaching and Research

Research
Education
References

Research

There are relatively few research studies on group treatment and group work in occupational therapy. This should not be surprising, because the field is young and there are many problems in conducting research with groups. A group is, by definition, a dynamic entity that involves a number of interpersonal variables that defy the usual controls applied to research studies. In outcome studies, for instance, the standard controls for error are practically impossible to impose, since each group may be expected to respond differently because of its unique developmental context. The fact that no two groups are alike poses problems of replication. Furthermore, ethical and professional considerations complicate research design and restrict research opportunities. Despite these problems, important new research studies in occupational therapy group work were recently published, and several of these deserve special consideration.

Schwartzberg, Howe and McDermott (1982) undertook a descriptive study of three treatment group formats in an acute in-patient psychiatric unit of a general hospital. The researchers sought to identify and analyze patterns in the quality and quantity of verbal interaction in these groups. The groups studied were a community group meeting, a self-expression group that was a combination of task and process-oriented occupational therapy group treatment, and an open occupational therapy group in which patients could choose and carry out individual activities. Results showed that the open occupational therapy group had a significantly greater amount of person-to-person communication than did the other two group formats and that this group also had a smaller number of patients who neither spoke nor were addressed. We may infer from this study that differences in quality and quantity of interaction are related to differences in group format.

Kremer, Nelson and Duncombe (1984) studied chronic psychiatric patients engaged in three different group activities in a community day treatment program. Patients were randomly assigned to three groups: a cooking group, a craft activity group, and a sensory awareness activity group. After the group activity, each patient rated the affective meaning of the activity, using Osgood's semantic differential scale. Results showed some differences in the affective meaning of these three activities. This research study constitutes a beginning in the long process of documenting the meaning that a particular patient population assigns to the group action.

Henry, Nelson and Duncombe (1984) examined the affective responses of subjects to having or not having freedom of choice in engaging in a particular activity. In addition, the researchers compared the responses of subjects to completing the activity in an individual and a group setting. The subjects in this study were college students. The results indicated that there was a significant relation between choice and affective meaning for activities in the group setting. Subjects in the group with no choice of activity rated themselves as feeling significantly less powerful than those in the group that had a choice of activity. This finding supports one of the basic assumptions of the functional group; specifically, members should be included in selecting and adapting the activity of the group.

New and creative ways need to be developed to evaluate the outcome of different types of group treatment. Descriptive and phenomenological research designs may prove to be better suited for evaluating the complex variables found in outcome studies. Because of the increasing concern with accountability in the health care professions, research on the outcome of various approaches to treatment has become especially important. Research can also help us describe more accurately the processes within groups: cohesion, feedback, support, structure, and so on. We need greater clarification of these concepts so that they can be better understood by both practitioners and researchers. The information generated through research is crucial if therapists are to transcend the limitations of one particular model and make discerning choices among treatment alternatives.

Education

It is fitting that we should end this book with a section on education, since we have been working in the field of occupational therapy education for many years. In part, the lack of educational material in the field motivated us to undertake this book. Over 25 years ago, in the proceedings of the Allenberry Conference, West (1959) reported on how group process was being taught in the occupational therapy curriculum of the time. According to a survey, the most common method used to teach group process was lecture and discussion. No research has been done on how this has changed over the years.

The education for group work in occupational therapy should be oriented to the occupational context of the field. The group process and group tasks are closely related to concepts of human occupation and adaptation. An understanding of activity evaluation and analysis is indispensable to leaders and will enable them to guide the group to achieve specific treatment goals. However, an intellectual understanding of the functional group is not enough. It is essential that lecture or discussion be combined with a laboratory experience through which the student can internalize what has been learned intellectually. Only through direct experience can the student realize the power of a group and see how this power can be used to promote healing or cause trauma and pain. Through personal experience, the student develops an awareness of the importance of group acceptance, the difficulty of revealing feelings, especially positive feelings, and the courage necessary to test reality and change specific ways of behaving. Participating in a group activity as a group member provides a different experience from participation in a discussion about the activity. Finally, to view the role of the leader from the vantage point of a member provides future leaders with an understanding of the unrealistic expectations that members often have of their group leader.

239

In the supervised clinical experience, the therapist assumes the role of leader for the first time. This is often a difficult experience, and the support of a supervisor or co-therapist can be invaluable. The supervisor may also provide the feedback necessary to learn from experience. New therapists are frequently impatient with the pace of development in their groups, not realizing that it is difficult for a group to develop mutual concern and caring. The result is too-frequent leader intervention and a prolonged dependency of the members upon their leader. An experienced co-therapist or supervisor helps the new therapist to be aware of such problems.

References

Henry, A., Nelson, D., and Duncombe, L. (1984). Choice making in group and individual activity. American Journal of Occupational Therapy 38(4): 245–251.

Kremer, E., Nelson, D., and Duncombe, L. (1984). Effects of selected activities on affective meaning in psychiatric patients. American Journal of Occupational Therapy 38(8): 522–528.

Schwartzberg, S. L., Howe, M. C., and McDermott, A. (1982). A comparison of three treatment group formats for facilitating social interaction. Occupational Therapy in Mental Health: A Journal of Psychosocial Practice and Research 2(4): 1–16.

West, W. L. (ed.) (1959). Changing Concepts and Practices in Psychiatric Occupational Therapy. New York: American Occupational Therapy Association.

Index

Page numbers followed by *f* indicate illustrations; *t* following a page number indicates tabular material.

248